IELTS
Ideas
and Vocabulary

CAROLYN CATT

ISBN 0-476-00073-4

Published by:

Catt Publishing

Copies available from:

CATT PUBLISHING
24 Stenness Avenue
Somerfield
Christchurch 8002
New Zealand
Email: cattpublishing@ihug.co.nz

acknowledgements

The author would like to thank her students for
their enthusiasm and support in trialling these materials.

Printed for the Publisher at:
The Caxton Press, Christchurch, New Zealand

contents

introduction

TO THE STUDENTS

This book can be used for self-study on your own, or in a class with other students.

The exercises in the book will help you prepare for the topics and ideas that you may be asked to talk about in the speaking test or to write about in task 2 of the writing test. The same topics and ideas may also occur in the listening test and in the academic module reading test.

The main aims of the book are

- to help you to form your own opinions about a range of topics
- to increase your understanding of topics that you may read or hear about in the IELTS examination
- to develop your vocabulary so that you can understand and express ideas on a range of topics

TO THE TEACHER

IELTS Ideas and Vocabulary can be used in self-study mode by learners working alone, or in the classroom by teachers working with groups of learners. The Teacher's Notes section provides suggestions on tasks and classroom management techniques to provide opportunities for communicative and collaborative work in the classroom.

When preparing for the IELTS test, many students encounter difficulties in their expression and comprehension of ideas on frequently encountered IELTS topics because

- they have little knowledge about those topics
- they have insufficient language relating to those topics

This lack of information and also of topic-specific language can cause them problems in both their productive skills (speaking and writing) and also in the receptive skills (listening and reading).

IELTS Ideas and Vocabulary was written to address these difficulties. The materials present learners with ideas relevant to common IELTS topics; they also support learners in the development and expression of their own ideas and opinions. The units include texts and tasks that

- introduce useful vocabulary
- personalise the topic for the learners
- focus on the learners' own cultures
- provide both speaking and writing practice
- present information or ideas on the topic
- encourage the learners to formulate their own ideas and opinions
- support the learners' own research of the topic

The units generally become progressively more demanding from unit 1 to unit 13 and there is some recycling of language between the units. Teachers may, nevertheless, prefer to work through the units in a different order and will find that there is no real problem in adopting this approach.

DISCLAIMER

The materials in this book are not taken from the IELTS examination.

UNIT 1 food

EXERCISE 1

STAPLE FOODS

A Match the staple foods in the left-hand column below with the countries in the right-hand column:

Staple Foods	Countries
bread	Paraguay
potatoes	China
rice	France
cassava/manioc	Mexico
corn	Ireland

B What is the staple food of your own country? Is there more than one staple food? How many times a week do you eat your staple food(s)?

EXERCISE 2

COOKING METHODS

A Tick the cooking methods you can use with your own favourite staple food from the list below:

baking	roasting	steaming
boiling	stir frying	grilling

deep frying (frying in a lot of oil)

shallow frying (frying in a small amount of oil)

B Which of the cooking methods is least healthy? Which is most healthy? Why?

C Which cooking method does the following paragraph describe and what staple food does 'them' refer to?

First you wash them carefully and dry them. You can rub a little oil on the outside, if you want. You heat an oven to about 180 degrees centigrade and put them in the middle of the oven. Depending on how big they are, they will be ready to eat in about 35 to 50 minutes. You can serve them with butter and salt, with grated cheese or different sauces.

EXERCISE 3 Write a paragraph describing how to cook your favourite staple food.

EXERCISE 4

INGREDIENTS AND TASTES

A Write the 5 groups of ingredients in the left-hand column below, next to the related taste:

Groups of ingredients:

soya sauce, salt   sugar, honey   tofu, flour   chilli   cheese, butter, cream

Ingredients	Tastes	Foods
_____	sweet	de´sserts, _____
_____	spicy	_____
_____	rich	_____
_____	salty	_____
_____	bland	_____

B   Which of the tastes above do you like most?

C   In the right-hand column, write 1 or 2 examples of food with the tastes in the list above. Mark the word stress. We have given you one example – de´sserts.

EXERCISE 5   a) What things do you think this person likes eating?

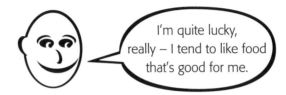

I'm quite lucky, really – I tend to like food that's good for me.

b) Check your ideas with the information below about what he likes eating:

I prefer savoury food to sweet food; and I dislike rich food with lots of cream or butter in it. I enjoy simple, quite plain food – for example, lightly grilled fish with steamed vegetables. Some people consider that type of food to be bland and boring, but I think that if you use really good, fresh ingredients, it can be very tasty. I also like spicy food, things like curries with spices such as cardamom and coriander – but nothing too hot and I'm not keen on a lot of chilli. Fortunately, I don't enjoy fatty foods – things with a lot of oil or animal fat in them – so I don't eat much fried food.

EXERCISE 6   Write a paragraph about the types of food you like and dislike, using language from Exercises 1, 2, 3 and 4.

EXERCISE 7   **DRINKS**

Look at the list of drinks below. Circle the ones that you like to drink. Put a tick next to the ones that your parents like to drink.

black tea	green tea	herbal tea	coffee
hot water	hot chocolate	cold milk	cold water
milk shakes	fruit juice	beer	wine
spirits (e.g. whisky, rum, mao tai, sake)		soft drinks (e.g. Coca Cola, fruit drinks)	

Do you and your parents like to drink the same things? If not, why not?

EXERCISE 8   **HEALTH PROBLEMS**

What health problems do you think may result from eating or drinking the following:

Food/Drink	**Possible health problems**
sweet foods	_____
spicy foods	_____
rich food	_____
salty food	_____
soft drinks	_____
alcoholic drinks	_____

YOUR CULTURE

Look at the sentences below. Tick any that are true about your country and change the others so that they are also true about your country.

a) Children are getting fatter.

b) More and more people are eating fast food such as burgers and chips.

c) Most people eat their evening meals sitting in front of the television.

d) People only eat traditional meals at festivals.

e) Men and women share the cooking equally.

f) Women prefer to cook frozen ready meals instead of preparing food from basic ingredients.

g) People are eating more and more dairy foods such as butter and ice cream.

h) People enjoy eating food from all over the world.

i) People who live in cities eat out in restaurants 2 or 3 times a week.

j) Only rich people can afford to buy good quality food.

Give reasons for the above statements. For example:

a) Children are getting fatter because they eat a lot of junk food such as chocolate and soft drinks.

HOMEWORK
UNIT 1

Find more information about the food in your country from a tourist guide book, an encyclopedia or from one of these websites:

For Japanese students, look at this website: **www.hirokoskitchen.com**

For all Asian students, look at this website: **www.asiarecipe.com**

For Brazilian students, look at this website: **www.brazilbrazil.com**

For all nationalities, look at these websites: **www.travel.yahoo.com**
(then look at the map under 'Destination Guides' and click on your area of the world – eg. Asia – then click on your country, then click on 'Dining')

www.topics-mag.com
(then click on 'World of food')

Then choose webpages to read. When you find a useful webpage, print it out.

NB Do not memorise any texts you find. It will not help you in the IELTS examination. Only use the texts for information, for reading practice and to extend your vocabulary.

UNIT 2 family

EXERCISE 1   **RELATIVES**

A   Which of the following are blood relatives and which are relatives by marriage? Write BR (blood relative) or RM (relative by marriage) next to each one. (Be careful, some could be a BR <u>and</u> a RM.)

mother	father	brother	sister
stepmother	stepfather	stepbrother	stepsister
mother-in-law	father-in-law	brother-in-law	sister-in-law
aunt	uncle	nephew	niece
cousin	grandmother	grandfather	

B   Mark the word stress for the vocabulary above.

C   How many of these blood relatives and relatives by marriage do you have? Put a number next to each relative.

D   What are the advantages of living in a large family? What are the advantages of living in a small family? Make notes below:

Large family	Small family

EXERCISE 2   **FAMILIES**

Match the following statements with the pictures below.

a) I'm an only child.   b) I have an older brother.   c) I have a younger sister.

d) I'm the youngest child in my family.   e) I'm the oldest child in my family.

f) I'm the third child.   g) I live in a nuclear family.   h) I live with my extended family.

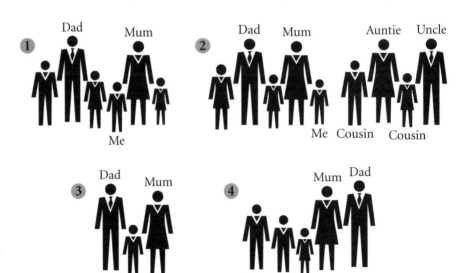

8

EXERCISE 3   Mark the word stress for the following vocabulary and circle the correct word class (noun, verb, adjective) next to each word. Check you understand their meaning.

single	verb / adjective	engaged	noun / adjective
married	noun / adjective	separated	noun / adjective
divorced	noun / adjective	adopt	verb / adjective
widow	noun / adjective	widower	noun / adjective
half-brother	noun / adjective	half-sister	noun / adjective

EXERCISE 4   Look at sentences a) to j) below and change them so that they are true about you. Add 2 more sentences about your family.

a)   I'm married. I got married 2 years ago.

b)   I have no nephews or nieces.

c)   I don't have a father-in-law or any other 'in-laws' because I'm single!

d)   I have 3 grandparents – two grandmothers and one grandfather.

e)   My grandfather is a widower.

f)   I have a half-brother.

g)   I have two stepchildren.

h)   I live with my extended family.

i)   I'm an only child.

j)   My aunt and uncle have adopted 2 children.

k)   _____

l)   _____

EXERCISE 5   In your opinion, which of the following is the best place for old people to live? Why?

i)   with a son and daughter-in-law   ii) with a daughter and son-in-law

iii) in a retirement home   iv) alone in their own home

v) (other) _____

EXERCISE 6   Write a paragraph about your family using language from Exercises 1, 2, 3 and 4.

EXERCISE 7   **VOCABULARY**

A   What do the following parts of words mean? Match them with their meanings:

Word Parts	Meanings
solo- (e.g. soloist)	one
bi- (e.g. bicycle)	alone, one
mono- (e.g. monoplane)	many
poly- (e.g. polygon)	two

B   Find and underline 3 words in Exercise 8 that start with 'solo-', 'bi-', 'mono-' or 'poly-'. Guess their meanings before you check them in a dictionary.

EXERCISE 8   **YOUR CULTURE**

Answer these questions about your country:

a) Is divorce common? What percentage of marriages end in divorce? Is divorce increasing? If so, why?

b) Does the government help solo parents? If so, how?

c) What age do most people marry? Is it different for boys and for girls? If so, why?

d) Do many people in your country adopt children?

e) Is bigamy/polygamy a crime in your country?

f) How do most people meet their marriage partners? Are arranged marriages common?

g) Describe a traditional wedding in your country.

h) How do married couples celebrate their wedding anniversaries? Which anniversary is most important (e.g. their 50th anniversary)?

i) How many children do most people have? Is the number increasing or decreasing? Why?

j) Is the number of old people increasing or decreasing? Why?

Homework
UNIT 2

Find more information about families and weddings in your country from an encyclopaedia or from a website on the internet.

For information about weddings, look at this website:

www.world-wedding-traditions.net
(then click on the area of the world that you live in – e.g. Asia – and then click on the name of your country)

For other information, you can go to a search engine such as **www.google.com** and type in keywords; e.g.

"marriage age in China"	"marriage age in Russia"
"arranged marriages"+Japan	"arranged marriages"+Taiwan
"birth rate"+Malaysia	"family life"+China
	"divorce rate"+Thailand

(Be careful to use + and " " as shown above).

Then choose webpages to read. When you find a useful webpage, print it out.

NB Do not memorise any texts you find. It will not help you in the IELTS examination. Only use the texts for information, for reading practice and to extend your vocabulary.

UNIT 3 clothing

EXERCISE 1

FASHION

A

Put the following vocabulary into the table below:

silk	short-sleeved	cotton	shirt	blouse
polo-neck	wool	suit	jacket	lycra
skirt	polyester	trousers	full-length	V-neck
close-fitting	linen	morning suit	sweater	round-neck
nylon	long-sleeved	down	flared	sleeveless
	sweatshirt		viscose	

Type of fabric (noun)	Type of clothing (noun)	Style of clothing (adjective)

B

Tick the fabrics in the left-hand column above that are synthetic (man-made).

C

Look at the following list of clothing. Tick any that are fashionable now. Change the other clothing to describe what is fashionable now.

    i) Full-length linen skirts   ii) Sleeveless down jackets

    iii) V-neck wool sweaters   iv) Close-fitting silk shirts

          v) Flared lycra trousers

EXERCISE 2

COLOURS AND CLOTHING

A

Add any more colours to this list that you know:

pink, pale blue, white, black, red, grey, dark green, blue, navy, maroon, purple ......

B

On the lines below, write the colours that are most usual in your culture for the following types of clothing:

    business suits _____

    a wedding dress _____

    clothes for women going to a wedding _____

    clothes for men going to a wedding _____

    baby clothes for boys _____

    baby clothes for girls _____

    clothes for people going to a funeral _____

    uniforms_____

EXERCISE 3   Write a short description of the clothes you are wearing now, using language from Exercises 1 and 2.

EXERCISE 4   To what extent do you agree with the following statements? Say why you agree or disagree.

    a)   People who have pale skins do not look good in yellow clothes.

    b)   People with black hair look good in black clothes.

    c)   People with blonde hair look good in red clothes.

    d)   People with blonde hair and blue eyes look good in white clothes.

    e)   People with red hair look good in red clothes.

    f)   Red clothes are lucky.

    g)   Green clothes are unlucky.

    h)   Old people should wear black clothes.

    i)   Young children should wear brightly coloured clothes.

    j)   Babies should wear pale-coloured clothes.

EXERCISE 5   Circle the item of clothing in each line below that is incorrect.

Casual clothing: jeans, polyester tracksuit, trainers, cotton T-shirt, silk bowtie

Formal women's clothing: high-heeled shoes, silk dress, wool suit, cap, silk blouse

Formal men's clothing: wool suit, cotton sweatshirt, silk tie, dinner jacket, cotton shirt

EXERCISE 6   **YOUR CLOTHES**

Answer these questions about yourself:

a) What colours do you prefer to wear? Why?

b) Describe the clothes you wear (the type of clothing, the fabrics and the styles):

- to go to your work or your place of study
- to relax at home
- to go out with friends (e.g. to a bar, to the cinema etc.)
- to go to parties

c) How often do you buy new clothes?

d) Do you prefer to go shopping alone or with another person? Why?

e) Do you or your family make your own clothes (by sewing or knitting)? Why/Why not?

f) Do you or your family have your clothes made by other people? Why/Why not?

EXERCISE 7   **UNIFORMS**

A   Tick the people in the list below who normally wear uniforms in your country.

the police	primary school children	secondary school children
nurses	workers in food factories	shop assistants
doctors	postal workers	bus drivers
	hotel workers	

B   Describe a uniform that people in your country wear.

C   Look at the list of reasons below as to why people wear uniforms. After each reason, write the different people who wear a uniform for that reason:

- so that people can quickly recognise what job they do _____

- so that they look smart _____

- so that they are clean and hygienic _____

- so that they do not try to compete with each other to
  look fashionable _____

- so that they feel that they are part of a team (i.e. a group
  of people working together) _____

Add any other reasons why people wear uniforms in your country.

EXERCISE 8   **YOUR CULTURE**

Answer the following questions about your own country:

a) Is there a traditional costume that women wear? If so, describe it and say when they wear it.

b) Is there a traditional costume that men wear? If so, describe it and say when they wear it.

c) Who wears traditional clothing most – men or women? Why?

d) Do people in different parts of your country wear different types of clothing? If so, why?

e) In what ways are the clothes that you wear different from the clothes your parents or grandparents wear?

Homework
UNIT 3

Find more information about clothing from a tourist guide book, an encyclopedia or from one of these websites:

For Asian students, look at this website: **www.asiarecipe.com**
                                              (then type 'clothes' in the search box)

For all students, look at this website: **www.costumes.org**
                                           *(then click on 'Ethnic Dress', then
                                           click on the area of the world that
                                           you live in – e.g. Asia – then look at*
OR   *any interesting webpages)*

Go to a search engine such as **www.google.com** and type in keywords; e.g.

        "traditional dress"+Korea   "traditional dress"+India

(Be careful to use + and " " as shown above).

Then choose webpages to read. When you find a useful webpage, print it out.

NB   Do not memorise any texts you find. It will not help you in the IELTS examination. Only use the texts for information, for reading practice and to extend your vocabulary.

UNIT 4 housing

EXERCISE 1 **VOCABULARY**

A Match the word parts below with their meanings:

Word Parts	Meanings
single- (e.g. single-minded)	noun
semi- (e.g. semi-circle)	under, below, less than
-less (e.g. hopeless)	many
sub- (e.g. substandard)	without
urb- (e.g. urban)	half
-ship (e.g. friendship)	city
multi- (e.g. multi-talented)	one, only, alone

B Memorise the meanings and their associated word parts and then test yourself.

C Quickly scan this unit and put a circle round any words you can find with 'single', 'semi', 'less', 'sub', 'urb', 'ship' or 'multi'. (There are 10 words in Exercises 2, 3, 5 and 6).

EXERCISE 2 Match the following descriptions of types of housing with the pictures below:

a) I have a small apartment on the 8th floor of a multi-storey apartment block.

b) I grew up in a semi-detached house.

c) We live in a single-storey house.

d) My family live in a terraced house.

e) I live in a detached house.

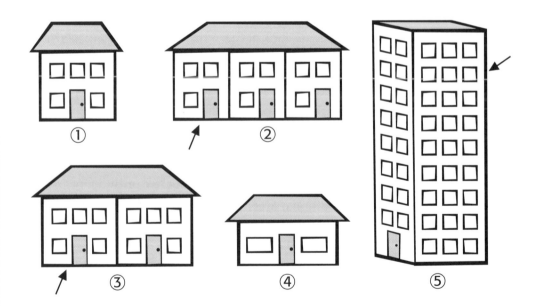

EXERCISE 3 **DESCRIBING HOMES**

A Read the following text describing someone's house. Do you like and dislike the same things as the speaker?

Paragraph 1

> I rent an apartment, but I want to move out because it's got very small windows, so it's quite dark, which I find depressing, and because there is so little fresh air, it's airless in summer. All the rooms feel cramped because they're small and they've got quite low ceilings. There's too much furniture, so it feels very cluttered, and the décor is very old-fashioned. It's really horrible.

Paragraph 2

> What I'd like is a modern apartment with large rooms, high ceilings and only a few pieces of modern furniture; that way, it would feel spacious. And I'd like big picture windows that you could throw open in summer, so that the whole place would be light and airy. I think a house like that would really lift my spirits and make me feel happier.

B   Find the words in paragraph 1 that are listed in the left hand column below. Underline them in paragraph 1:

Paragraph 1	Paragraph 2
very small windows	big picture windows
dark	_____
airless	_____
cramped	_____
low ceilings	_____
cluttered	_____
old-fashioned	_____

C   Now find the words in paragraph 2 that mean the *opposite* of the words you underlined in paragraph 1. Write them in the right hand column above (we have done the first one for you).

EXERCISE 4   **YOUR HOME**

Write one paragraph about your own home and another paragraph about your ideal home, using the prompts below and language from Exercises 2 and 3.

    a)   What type of housing do you live in?
    b)   What do you like about your home and what do you dislike about it?
    c)   What would your perfect house be like?

EXERCISE 5   Put the following vocabulary into the table below and mark the word stress:

the countryside	to rent	stone	urban areas
to pay a mortgage	mud	wood	to own
the suburbs	concrete	the city centre	brick

Areas to live	Building materials	Home ownership

EXERCISE 6

YOUR CULTURE

Try to answer the following questions, using vocabulary from Exercises 2, 3 and 5:

a) What type of housing is most common in urban areas in your country?

b) What type of housing is most common in rural areas in your country?

c) What percentage of people in your country own their own homes and what percentage rent their homes?

d) Are most rented homes owned by the government or by private landlords?

e) Do people of different ages prefer to live in different types of housing? Why?

f) Do people of different ages prefer to live in the city centre, in urban areas, in the suburbs or in the countryside? Why?

g) What materials (concrete, wood, brick etc) is modern housing made of in your country?

h) What materials (wood, brick, mud etc) are traditional buildings made of in your country?

i) Do cities in your country have any homeless people (people who live on the street)? Does anyone help them (e.g. the government or charities)? If so, how?

j) Are there any other housing problems in your country? If so, why?

Homework
UNIT 4

Find information about famous buildings in your country from an encyclopedia or from a website:

For Asian students, look at this website: **www.orientalarchitecture.com**
(then click on your country, then click on a famous building or site)

For other students, go to a search engine such as **www.google.com** and type in keywords; e.g.

"famous architecture"+"in Brazil"

Find information about housing in your country from an encyclopedia or from a website:

Go to a search engine such as **www.google.com** and type in keywords; e.g.

"Japanese architecture"+housing   "Indonesian architecture"+housing

(Be careful to use + and " " as shown above).

Then choose webpages to read. When you find a useful webpage, print it out.

NB Do not memorise any texts you find. It will not help you in the IELTS examination. Only use the texts for information, for reading practice and to extend your vocabulary.

UNIT 5 pets

EXERCISE 1 **VOCABULARY OF OPPOSITES**

A Check you understand the meanings of the vocabulary in the left-hand column below and mark the word stress.

Vocabulary	**Opposites**
responsible (adjective)	_____
practical (adjective)	_____
affectionate (adjective)	_____
faithful (adjective)	_____
dependent (adjective)	_____
expensive (adjective)	_____
legal (adjective)	_____
treat well (verb + 'well')	_____
behave well (verb + 'well')	_____
obedient (adjective)	_____
easy to train ('easy'+ 'to'+ infinitive)	_____

B Write the opposites of the vocabulary in the right-hand column above and mark the word stress.

C Quickly scan this unit and underline the above vocabulary and its opposites. (There are 9 words in Exercises 3, 4, 5 and 6 below.)

EXERCISE 2 **POPULAR PETS**

A Tick the animals in the list below that people keep as pets in your country:

dogs   cats   goldfish   hamsters   canaries

B Add any other pets that people in your country like to keep.

EXERCISE 3 **PET CHARACTERISTICS**

A What are the 6 most popular pets in your country? Write them in the left-hand column below in order of popularity (1 is most popular and 6 is least popular).

Pets	**Characteristics**
i) _____	_____
ii) _____	_____
iii) _____	_____
iv) _____	_____
v) _____	_____
vi) _____	_____

B Choose characteristics from the list below and write them next to the correct animal in the right-hand column above (you may have more than 1 characteristic for each type of pet and you can use opposites of the characteristics listed below – See Exercise 1 for the opposites).

Characteristics:

faithful	affectionate	cuddly	fun
useful	amusing	interesting	quiet
unusual	easy to care for	obedient	easy to train
clean	independent	good company	brave
	inexpensive to care for		

C Add more characteristics for each pet if you can.

D Write a description of the type of pet you like best, using vocabulary from Exercises 1, 2 and 3.

EXERCISE 4 Which pets are most suitable for the following groups of people? Why?

toddlers (young children aged between 1 and $2\frac{1}{2}$ years old)

single working people who live alone

young children aged 6-12

elderly people living alone

EXERCISE 5 **PROBLEMS**

A Look at the following statements about problems with pets. Tick any that are true about your country and change others so that they are also true about your country.

i) Dogs and cats get lost from their homes and live wild in city streets.

ii) Dogs often misbehave – they may attack people, they may bark a lot or they may run in front of cars.

iii) Dogs defecate on streets and in parks, spreading diseases.

iv) Owners cannot afford to look after their pets so they abandon them on the street.

v) Cats make a lot of noise at night and keep people awake.

vi) Irresponsible owners go away on holiday and leave their pets for days without food or water.

B How do you think these problems can be reduced or solved? Write a solution for each problem above.

C Look at the text which follows and

i) Check which problems in the list in Exercise 5A above are mentioned in the text.

ii) Check if the text has similar ideas to yours about how to reduce or solve the problems.

In many countries people who own dogs have to buy a licence for that dog and it has to wear a collar with the licence number on it. That way, if it gets lost or if it is left on the street, the owner can be found. Any dogs whose owners cannot be found after 2 weeks are destroyed (i.e. killed). The dog licence systems also means that if owners mistreat their dog in any way, they may have their dog licence taken away from them so that they cannot own a dog again.

In some cities it is illegal for dogs to be in public places unless they are on a lead – in that way the owner can control the dog and prevent it from attacking people. It also means that any dog that is not on a lead can be picked up by dog control officers, so dogs cannot live wild on the streets of a city; and if dogs are on leads, owners can see where their dog defecates and they can then remove the mess using plastic bags so that other people are not affected.

Many cities also have laws about how much noise dogs can make – if barking dogs disturb the neighbours, the dog's owner can be fined and sometimes the dog may be trained not to bark or it may even have its bark removed in an operation.

It is, of course, impractical to put cats on leads as they are much more difficult to control than dogs, but owners should bring them in at night and not let them out until morning.

EXERCISE 6   **YOUR CULTURE**

Try and answer the following questions about your country:

a)   What animals are people not allowed to have as pets in your country? Why?

b)   What percentage of households in your country have pets?

c)   What laws are there about keeping pets such as dogs and cats in your country?

d)   What laws are there about keeping dangerous animals as pets (e.g. poisonous snakes, poisonous spiders, tigers, bears etc)?

e)   Do more people today have pets than in your grandparents' time? If so, why?

f)   How much money do people spend on their pets? Is it too much?

g)   Why do people like to have pets?

Homework
UNIT 5

Find more information about pets from an encyclopedia or from a website:

For information about looking after pets, look at this website:

www.spca.bc.ca *(then click on 'Animal care,' then click on the different animals)*

For information about pets in your country, go to a search engine such as **www.google.com** and type in keywords, including the name of your city, your capital city or your country; e.g.

"popular pets"+Seoul   "popular pets"+Japan

(Be careful to use + and " " as shown above).

Then choose webpages to read. When you find a useful webpage, print it out.

NB Do not memorise any texts you find. It will not help you in the IELTS examination. Only use the texts for information, for reading practice and to extend your vocabulary.

UNIT 6 cities

EXERCISE 1   **VOCABULARY OF QUANTITY**

A   Put the following expressions in order of quantity from most to least. Write them in the column headed 'Quantity':

Quantity

A few (cars)   _____

Quite a number of (cars)   _____

No (cars)   _____

One or two (cars)   _____

Several (cars)   _____

A large number of (cars)   _____

B   Tick the correct answer to complete this sentence:

All the quantity expressions are followed by …

     i)   an uncountable noun (e.g. money, bread)

     ii)   a singular countable noun (e.g. vehicle, house)

     iii)   a plural countable noun (e.g. vehicles, houses)

EXERCISE 2   **FACILITIES**

A   Write the following vocabulary under the correct headings in the chart below and mark the word stress:

Vocabulary

office block   crèche   synagogue   secondary school   shopping mall

mosque   market   university   temple   primary school

factory   church   kindergarten

Places of worship	Business premises	Educational institutions	Child care facilities

B   Tick the facilities in the chart above that your home town or city has.

C   Write a short paragraph about the facilities in your home town or city using the quantity expressions from Exercise 1.

D   Decide which are the 5 most important facilities for a town and why.

EXERCISE 3   **AGE GROUPS**

A   Complete the statements on the next page by inserting the following figures on the lines:

1	2	3	6	7	12	12	13	18
19	20	29	33	40	59	60	65	70

Babies are infants under the age of ____ months.

Toddlers are aged between____ and ____ ¹/₂ years old.

Teenagers are aged between ____ and ____ years old.

People in their 20s are aged between ____ and ____ .

People in their early 30s are aged between 30 and ____ .

People in their mid 40s are aged between 44 and 4___ .

People in their late 50s are aged between 5___ and ____ .

Middle aged people are between ____ and ____ years old.

Pensioners/retired people have finished working and/or are aged ____ years old.

The elderly are aged over ____ years old.

The word 'child' is generally used about a boy or girl aged between ____ and ____ years old.

The word 'adult' is generally used about someone who is over ____ years of age.

B Make sentences using the age group vocabulary above. Try to write about yourself, your family or your culture.

e.g. When I was a **toddler**, I broke my arm.

e.g. My parents are **in their early 40s**.

EXERCISE 4 **LEISURE TIME**

A Mark the word stress on the vocabulary in the middle column below, then choose the best heading from the following list and write it on the line at the top of the middle column:

Heading 1: Fun activities

Heading 2: Leisure activities

Heading 3: Leisure facilities

Frequency of use	_____	Age groups
_____	museums	_____
_____	cinemas	_____
_____	opera houses	_____
_____	art galleries	_____
_____	concert halls	_____
_____	theatres	_____
_____	swimming pools	_____
_____	sports stadiums	_____
_____	parks	_____

B In the left-hand column above, under 'Frequency of use', write the number of times you use the different leisure facilities (e.g. once a week, twice a month, 3 times a year, never, occasionally, every day, every Saturday). Try not to use 'often' or 'sometimes'.

C In the right-hand column above, under 'Age groups', write the age groups that use the different leisure facilities most (children, teenagers, university students, people in their 20s, people in their late 40s, retired people, etc.).

D Write 2 paragraphs. In the first paragraph, write about the facilities you use most frequently. In the second paragraph, write about the facilities that an age group (not your own age group) uses and why they use those leisure facilities.

EXERCISE 5 **YOUR CULTURE**

Put a tick in the boxes below to show who is responsible for the facilities in towns and cities in your country.

Facilities	Local government	Central government	Private companies
city roads			
motorways			
multi-storey car parks			
city buses			
railways			
libraries			
banks			
airports			
hospitals			
apartment blocks			

Homework
UNIT 6

Find more information about your city's facilities from a tourist guide book, an encyclopedia or from a website:

For information about museums and art galleries, look at this website:

www.travel.yahoo.com *(then look at the map under 'Destination Guides' and click on your area of the world – eg. Africa – then click on your country, then select a city and press 'Go', then click on 'Attractions', then click on 'Museums and art galleries')*

OR

Go to a search engine such as **www.google.com** and type in keywords, including the name of your city or your capital city; e.g.

"museums"+Seoul   "libraries"+Delhi

(Be careful to use + and " " as shown above).

Then choose webpages to read. When you find a useful webpage, print it out.

NB Do not memorise any texts you find. It will not help you in the IELTS examination. Only use the texts for information, for reading practice and to extend your vocabulary.

UNIT 7 leisure

EXERCISE 1

A

VOCABULARY

Match the vocabulary in the left-hand column with the meaning in the right-hand column below:

Vocabulary	Meaning
A physical game	the opposite of the most important
An individual game	a game with 2 or more teams playing against each other
A competitive game	a square divided into 4 smaller squares
A team game	a job that does not involve moving the body
A sedentary job	a game where you try to beat another team or another person
A demanding job	a game that involves using the body
A quadrant	a game for one person or a game in which one person plays against one other person
The least important	a job that is difficult to do

B Mark the word stress on the vocabulary in the left-hand column above.

C Memorise the vocabulary and their meanings and then test yourself.

EXERCISE 2 Write a list of your 6 most favourite leisure activities (e.g. reading, surfing the internet, jogging, shopping, playing football, watching football etc.)

1. _____   4. _____

2. _____   5. _____

3. _____   6. _____

EXERCISE 3

A

PHYSICAL AND SEDENTARY ACTIVITIES

Organise the following leisure activities from most physical to most sedentary. Write the activities in order in the middle column:

Activities	Most physical	Points
playing table tennis	_____	Extremely physical – 5 points
sewing	_____	Very physical – 4 points
watching tv	_____	Fairly physical – 3 points
playing the piano	_____	Fairly sedentary – 2 points
running	_____	Very sedentary – 1 points
walking	_____	Extremely sedentary – 0 points

Most sedentary

B Look back at the list of your activities in Exercise 2. Give yourself points according to how physical or how sedentary your activities are. Are your leisure activities physical or sedentary?

EXERCISE 4   **THE IMPORTANCE OF PHYSICAL EXERCISE**

Look at the following statements and decide if they are true or false:

a) People who are physically active are less likely to suffer from heart disease.

b) People who are physically active are likely to get better quicker after an accident or a serious illness.

c) More and more people are suffering from illnesses such as diabetes because they are not physically active.

d) It is important to exercise 3 times a week for at least 20 minutes each time.

e) Children need to be physically active for their bodies to develop well.

EXERCISE 5   **SPORTS**

A   Put the following sports into the quadrant below:

football	bungy jumping	basketball	white water rafting
swimming	running	motor racing	skydiving
paragliding	mountain climbing	rugby	golf

	Competitive	**Non-competitive**
Team Sport		
Individual Sport		

B   Do you think that non-competitive sports are real sports? Or are they just adventure activities?

EXERCISE 6   What type of sport interests you most and why?

- Competitive team sports
- Non-competitive team sport
- Competitive individual sports
- Non-competitive individual sports

EXERCISE 7   Write about your own leisure activities, including vocabulary from Exercises 1 and 6.

EXERCISE 8   **YOUR CULTURE**

Answer the following questions about your country:

a) What are the favourite leisure activities of your generation? And of your parents' generation?

b) What is your country's national sport? Does your country do well at the Olympics in any particular sport(s)?

c) Why are some sports popular in some countries but not in other countries?

d) What sports in your country do wealthy people play and what sports do poorer people play? Why?

e) Do men play sport more than women? If so, why?

f) What physical exercise do children do at primary school? And at secondary school?

g) What are the possible positive effects of playing sports at school? And the possible negative effects?

h) What sports do you actively participate in and what sports do you watch?

i) Do you prefer to watch sports on television or in a sports stadium? Why?

j) What changes have there been in your country over the last 20-30 years in children's games and play activities?

k) In your country, do you think people are becoming less active? Why/why not?

Homework
UNIT 7

Find more information about sport and leisure activities in your city or country from a tourist guide book, an encyclopedia or from a website:

For information about leisure activities in your home town or city, look at these websites:

www.travel.yahoo.com *(then look at the map under 'Destination Guides' and click on your area of the world – eg. Europe – then click on your country, then select a city and press 'Go', then click on 'Entertainment')*

www.lonelyplanet.com/destinations *(in Box 1, click on your area of the world – e.g. Asia; in Box 2, click on your area/city and click on 'go', then click on 'Activities')*

For information about your national sport(s), go to a search engine such as **www.google.com** and type in keywords, including the name of your country; e.g.

"national sport"+Pakistan   "national sport"+China

(Be careful to use + and " " as shown above).

Then choose webpages to read. When you find a useful webpage, print it out.

NB Do not memorise any texts you find. It will not help you in the IELTS examination. Only use the texts for information, for reading practice and to extend your vocabulary.

8 transport

EXERCISE 1

A

VOCABULARY OF WORD PARTS

Match the word parts in the left-hand column below with their meanings in the middle column.

Word parts	Meanings	Example words
trans-	one	_____
port-	number	_____
bi-	between	_____
inter-	across	_____
urb-	carry	_____
mono-	city	_____
motor-	three	_____
numer-	engine	_____
tri-	two	_____

B

In the right-hand column above, write examples of words you know that contain the word parts and that have the same meanings.

EXERCISE 2

A

INTERCITY AND LOCAL TRANSPORT

List all the different forms of public and private transport in your home town or city and in your country – e.g. cars, ferries, planes, etc.

_____

_____

B

Read the text below about a mythical country called 'Palatonia'. Check if it talks about the same types of transport that you listed above.

1   Palatonia has a range of transport options for both local and intercity travel, all of which are cheap and efficient. Most large towns and cities offer a variety of public and private systems for local travel within and between urban and suburban areas. Public transport options include buses, trams, monorail and underground systems in most cities, with taxis

5   and rickshaws (both human-powered and motorised) available in the larger centres of population. The capital, Mafua, also has a network of small ferries that provide transport across the city harbour.

With regard to private transport options, the streets within all of Palatonia's major cities are not only designed for motorised vehicles, but also for bicycles. Designated bicycle lanes

10   provide a safe environment for cyclists and a large number of bicycle parking areas are available for use. Motorbikes and cars are also popular forms of commuter transport.

The movement of people between major towns and cities in Palatonia is by train (through the country's extensive rail network) by road (either using public service vehicles such as coaches and minibuses, or using private cars), by air (Palatonia has a total of 5 airlines

15   operating between its major centres) and by sea, using the numerous ferries that operate between the various islands.

C   Complete the mind map below about the different forms of public and private transport in Palatonia:

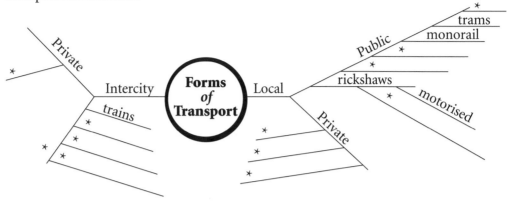

D   Look at the words in the left hand column below. Find and underline them in the text about Palatonia.

Match the vocabulary with the meanings in the right-hand column. (Check by re-reading the text).

Vocabulary	Meanings
range (line 1)	very many/a large number
options (line 1)	important/large
major (line 8)	variety
numerous (line 15)	different
various (line 16)	choices

EXERCISE 3   Draw a mind map of the local and intercity transport options for your home country. Then write 2 or more paragraphs about the mind map, using vocabulary from Exercises 1 and 2.

EXERCISE 4   **FACTORS AFFECTING CHOICE OF TRANSPORT**

A   Look at the adjectives in the left-hand column below. Mark the word stress.

Adjective	Noun
comfortable	_____
fast	_____
expensive	_____
private	_____
healthy	_____
easy	_____
convenient	_____
environmental	_____
safe	_____

B   In the right-hand column above, write the nouns for the adjectives in the left-hand column.

Mark the word stress for the nouns.

C   Practise saying the nouns and adjectives with the correct word stress.

EXERCISE 5　What forms of public or private transport do you use? Put the following factors in order of importance for you in your choice of transport to your work/place of study:

comfort	speed	expense
privacy	safety	health
ease of parking	convenience of use	environmental effect

EXERCISE 6　**YOUR CULTURE**

Try and answer the following questions about your home town or city:

- What is the most popular form of transport for these groups of people and why?

    the elderly　　business men and women

office workers　　factory workers　　mothers with young children

- How do children travel to school – by car, by public bus, by school bus, by bicycle, on foot? Why do they travel that way?

Homework
UNIT 8

Find more information about transport in your city or country from a tourist guide book, an encyclopedia or from a website:

For information about urban transport in your city, look at this website:

www.lonelyplanet.com/destinations *(in Box 1, click on your area of the world – e.g. Asia; in Box 2, click on your city and click on 'go', then click on 'Getting Around')*

For information about intercity transport in your country, look at these websites:

www.lonelyplanet.com/destinations *(in Box 1, click on your area of the world – e.g. Asia; in Box 2, click on your city and click on 'go', then click on 'Getting There and Away')*

www.travel.yahoo.com *(then look at the map under 'Destination Guides' and click on your area of the world – eg. Americas – then click on your country, then select a city and press 'Go', then click on 'Transportation')*

OR

Go to a search engine such as **www.google.com** and type in keywords, including the name of your city or country; e.g.

"public transport"+Shanghai　　"private car use"+Pakistan

(Be careful to use + and " " as shown above).

Then choose webpages to read. When you find a useful webpage, print it out.

NB Do not memorise any texts you find. It will not help you in the IELTS examination. Only use the texts for information, for reading practice and to extend your vocabulary.

UNIT 9 traffic

EXERCISE 1   **VOCABULARY OF QUANTITY**

A   Match the expressions of quantity to use with plural countable nouns (in the left-hand column) with the expressions of quantity to use with uncountable nouns such as 'bread', 'money', 'pollution' (in the right-hand column)

Quantity Expressions (countable nouns)	**Quantity Expressions (uncountable nouns)**
a large number of (cars)	a small amount of (pollution)
quite a number of (cars)	some (pollution)
several (cars)	a great deal of (pollution)
a few (cars)	no (pollution)
no (cars)	a fair amount of (pollution)

B   Quickly scan this unit and put a circle round any expressions of quantity you can find. (There are 9 expressions in Exercises 2, 3 and 4).

EXERCISE 2   **PROBLEMS AND EFFECTS**

A   Look at the following list of problems caused by transport. Tick any that are true in your country.

Problems	Health effects	Overall effect
Air pollution	_____	
Noise pollution	_____	
Traffic congestion	_____	_____
Traffic accidents	_____	

B   What are the effects of these problems? Write your ideas in the middle and right-hand columns above.

C   Check your ideas to Exercise 2B above by reading the following text:

> In my country, many cities are adversely affected by the large number of vehicles on the roads. For example, one problem is air pollution. In many towns and cities, the air pollution is so serious that a large number of people are suffering from respiratory diseases. In particular, children and the elderly are being affected by the poisonous fumes from car and bus exhausts. The noise of the traffic is a problem, too, as it causes loss of sleep and high levels of stress, which in turn leads to health problems such as heart disease and high blood pressure. Traffic congestion also causes stress and it wastes a great deal of time as people spend their time sitting in traffic jams. Traffic accidents are, of course, another problem because they result in injuries and even deaths. All-in-all, too many vehicles on our roads are causing a variety of health problems; and because people are unable to work while they are ill and the government has to spend money on health care, on roading and on policing the roads, the economy of the whole country is being affected negatively.

In the left-hand column below, write the verbs to match the meanings in the right-hand column:

Verb	Meaning
a) _____	To make something or someone able
b) _____	To make something longer
c) _____	To make something shorter
d) _____	To give someone the courage or confidence to do something.
e) _____	To make something wider
f) _____	To make something narrower
g) _____	To make something sure or certain
h) _____	To make something or someone stronger
i) _____	To make something or someone weaker

Make sentences for 5 of the verbs. Try to write about yourself or your country.

    e.g.   My new trousers were too long, so I <u>shortened</u> them.

    e.g.   The strikes by a large number of workers have <u>weakened</u> our economy.

EXERCISE 4

A

SOLUTIONS TO TRANSPORT PROBLEMS

Look at the following methods for local or central governments to reduce the negative impacts of vehicles. Put them in order from most effective/most useful to least effective/least useful:

a) They should encourage people to walk to work. Even a small amount of exercise every day would improve people's health. It would also reduce a fair amount of traffic.

b) They could widen roads so there is no traffic congestion.

c) They ought to strengthen the traffic rules so that people do not exceed the speed limit. This would reduce the large number of accidents.

d) They need to ensure that fares on public transport are much cheaper than the cost of car parks. This would encourage people to use public transport more and to leave their cars at home.

e) They might shorten parking spaces so that large cars cannot fit in them. This would encourage people to buy smaller cars and there would be a great deal less traffic congestion on the roads.

f) They should enable government workers to work flexible hours so the number of people travelling to work during the rush hour would fall.

g) They should create more cycle lanes that only bicycles can use. This would enable cyclists to travel safely to work or their place of study.

h) They should ban all old vehicles from the roads. This would remove a fair amount of air pollution as old cars produce more pollution.

B Think of other ways that local and central governments could reduce traffic on the roads. Write your ideas with sentences starting:

They could provide _____

They ought to increase _____

They need to reduce _____

They might prohibit _____

They should prevent _____

They could control _____

EXERCISE 5 Write about any traffic problems in your home town or city and suggest ways to solve the problems, using ideas from Exercises 1, 2, 3 and 4.

EXERCISE 6 **YOUR CULTURE**

Try and answer the following questions about your home town or city:

a) What percentage of families own a car?

b) What percentage of families own more than one car?

c) What percentage of families own a bicycle?

d) What percentage of families own more than one bicycle?

e) Do young people in your country use skate boards, roller blades or non-motorised scooters as forms of transport? Why/why not?

f) How much has traffic increased since your grandparents' time? Why?

Homework
UNIT 9

Find more information about traffic in your city or country from a website:

Go to a search engine such as **www.google.com** and type in keywords, including the name of your city or your country; e.g.

"car ownership"+Japan   "traffic problems"+Islamabad

(Be careful to use + and " " as shown above).

Then choose webpages to read. When you find a useful webpage, print it out.

NB Do not memorise any texts you find. It will not help you in the IELTS examination. Only use the texts for information, for reading practice and to extend your vocabulary.

UNIT 10 holidays

EXERCISE 1   **VOCABULARY OF STATUTORY HOLIDAYS**

A   In most countries there are some days when almost everyone has a holiday. These days are called bank holidays or statutory holidays. Which of the following days are statutory holidays in your country?

Christmas Day	Boxing Day	Good Friday
New Year's Day	National Day	May 1st	Independence Day

B   Add any other statutory holidays that you have in your country.

EXERCISE 2   **HOLIDAY ENTITLEMENT**

A   Look at the following information about holiday entitlement in a mythical country and answer these questions:

Is it the same in your country? If not, what is different?

In my country, most office and factory workers are entitled to 3 weeks' holiday a year plus statutory holidays – about 4 weeks in total. But more and more companies are giving their workers 4 weeks' holiday a year plus statutory holidays, especially for employees who have worked for the company for more than 3 years. Primary and secondary school teachers get much more – around 12 weeks a year plus statutory holidays – but they often complain that they don't really have it all as holiday because they have to prepare courses and even do administrative work during that time.

B   Write a short paragraph about holiday entitlement for workers in your country.

EXERCISE 3   **YOUR HOLIDAY ACTIVITIES**

Answer the following questions:

1. What do primary school children do in their holidays? Why?

   a) stay at home with their mother, grandmother or other relative

   b) stay at home with a nanny or babysitter

   c) go on a holiday programme organised by their school

   d) go to a kindergarten or crèche

2. What do secondary school children do in their holidays? Why?

   a) stay at home with their mother, grandmother or other relative

   b) go on a holiday programme organised by their school

   c) stay at home alone or spend time with friends

   d) get a holiday job

3. What do university students do in their holidays? Why?

    a) study

    b) go away on holiday

    c) stay at home and spend time with friends

    d) get a holiday job

4. Where do you spend your holidays? Why?

    a) in your own home

    b) in your own country but not in your own home

    c) overseas/abroad

5. Who do you prefer to spend your holiday with? Why?

    a) your family

    b) your friends

    c) with a group of people who you have not met before

    d) a mix of a) b) c).

    e) alone

EXERCISE 4   **DIFFERENT TYPES OF HOLIDAY**

A   Write the following vocabulary under the correct headings in the chart below:

Vocabulary

bed and breakfast	sightseeing	hotel
the homes of family/friends	shopping	relaxing on a beach
motel	hostel/backpacker's	campsite
visiting friends or relatives	playing sports	cruise ship

learning or practising a hobby (e.g. ski-ing, photography etc)

Accommodation	Holiday activity

B   Mark the word stress for the vocabulary in the chart above.

C   Add any other types of accommodation or holiday activity that you know.

EXERCISE 5   **YOUR PERFECT HOLIDAY**

Write about what would be a perfect holiday for you, using vocabulary and ideas from exercises 1, 2, 3 and 4. Include information about

        Where you would go (areas, cities, countries) and why

        Where you would stay (accommodation) and why

        What you would do (activities) and why

        Who you would go with and why

EXERCISE 6 **YOUR CULTURE**

Try to answer the following questions using vocabulary from Exercises 1, 2, 3 and 4.

a) What are the most popular destinations in your country for:

- Shopping
- Sightseeing
- Beach holidays

b) Which are the main holiday times for people in your country (name the season, the month or the festival)? Why are they the main holidays?

c) What sort of holidays are popular for people from your country:

- Where do they go (area, city, country) and why?
- Where do they stay (accommodation) and why?
- What do they do (activities) and why?
- Who do they go with and why?

d) What can visitors to your home town or city do and see there?

e) Are holidays in your country longer than they were in your grandparents' time? If so, why?

f) What did your grandparents do on their holidays? Was it different from today? If so, why?

g) Do you think some professionals – e.g. teachers or doctors – should have longer holidays than others? Why/why not?

Homework
UNIT 10

Find more information about holidays in your country from a tourist guide book, an encyclopedia or from a website:

For information about statutory holidays/festivals, look at this website:

> **www.lonelyplanet.com/destinations** *(in Box 1, click on your area of the world – e.g. Asia; in Box 2, click on your city and click on 'go', then click on 'Events')*

For information about sightseeing in your city or in your country, look at this website:

> **www.travel.yahoo.com** *(then look at the map under 'Destination Guides' and click on your area of the world – eg. Asia – then click on your country, then click on 'Attractions', then click on 'Places of interest')*

OR

Go to a search engine such as **www.google.com** and type in keywords, including the name of your city or your country; e.g.

> "Beach holidays"+China   "Sightseeing"+Hong Kong

(Be careful to use + and "" as shown above).

Then choose webpages to read. When you find a useful webpage, print it out.

NB Do not memorise any texts you find. It will not help you in the IELTS examination. Only use the texts for information, for reading practice and to extend your vocabulary.

UNIT 11 lifestyles

EXERCISE 1

VOCABULARY

A Match the vocabulary in the left-hand column with the definitions in the right-hand column below:

Vocabulary	**Definitions**
secure	how enjoyable life is
exhausted	the pay professional people receive for their work
nightlife	the number of crimes
pace	evening entertainment (e.g. nightclubs, cinema etc)
sense of community	feeling of loyalty and support between people in a group
crime rate	the way people live, based on what they can afford
housing	pressure/emotional strain
status	social or professional position
salary	safe/unlikely to fail
stress	speed
quality of life	extremely tired
standard of living	accommodation

B Mark the word stress for the vocabulary in the left-hand column above and write its word class (noun, adjective or noun phrase).

C Memorise the vocabulary and their meanings and then test yourself.

EXERCISE 2 Read the following texts and answer these questions:

    a) Which of these people has a high standard of living and which has a good quality of life?

    b) Which of these people would you prefer to be? Why?

1. I have a very well paid job as a senior manager in a large company. I own 3 cars and I live in a luxury apartment. The trouble is that I work 12 hours a day, 6 days a week and I'm always so exhausted when I get home from work that I don't see my family or friends very much; even on Sundays I never have enough energy to do anything except stay home. And I never have time to go away on holiday. I know I'm very lucky to have such a good job with so much money, but actually I hate the work – it's really boring.

2. I love my work – it's extremely interesting, but my salary is not very high, so I have to be careful with my money – I can't afford a new car and lots of clothes; but I work just 8 hours a day and I never feel stressed or tired at the end of the day, so I have lots of free time to do other things. I go out to see my family or friends every evening and we always have great fun together. And the weekends are always really good too, even if it's doing something cheap like having a picnic on the beach. I have a great life – I think I'm really lucky.

PRIORITIES

Put the following points in order from 1 to 12 (1 is most important to you, 12 is least important to you.)

a beautiful house/apartment	a good salary
a job with high status	a happy family life
overseas holidays	fashionable clothes
lots of free time	good food
good health	a secure job
good friends	an expensive car

Answer these questions:

- Would your parents put the points above in the same order as you? If not, why not?
- Would your grandparents put the points above in the same order as you? If not, why not?

Write a short paragraph about your priorities in life using vocabulary from Exercises 1, 2 and 3.

CITY LIFE AND COUNTRY LIFE

Put the following vocabulary into the gaps in the text below:

Vocabulary

clean air	variety of jobs	exciting nightlife	low crime rate
pace of life	traffic jams	pollution	sense of community
cost of living	shopping malls	stressful	long travel times to work
	healthy and safe environment		

I used to live in Tupu, in Palatonia. It's a very large city and has all the things you might expect in such a large city. One of the positive things is the large **1**_____ that are open 24 hours a day, so you can buy anything you want whenever you want; and the different entertainment options – Tupu has a really **2**_____. On the negative side, there is terrible **3**_____ because of all the cars; and there are terrible **4**_____ at rush hour – everyone complains about the **5**_____ every morning. A great many people move from the countryside into Tupu because there's a wide **6**_____ available in the city, but a lot of these people don't have the necessary skills. When they can't find a job, they turn to crime as a way of getting money. All-in-all, living in the city can be very **7**_____.

So, about 2 years ago, I moved to a village in the countryside about 70 kms outside Tupu. Life there is completely different. Of course, the **8**_____ is much slower, but that means people have time to talk to each other; and because everyone knows everyone else in the village they help each other – there is a real **9**_____. We don't have a police station in the village and people don't worry about locking their doors when they go out because there is a very **10**_____. And we have **11**_____ due to the small number of cars. All that makes it a very **12**_____ for children to grow up in. Although I miss Tupu's nightlife, it does have one advantage – I spend much less money than when I was living in the city; so the low **13**_____ in the countryside makes it easy to live on a small salary!

EXERCISE 6 Write a paragraph about your home town or city, using vocabulary from Exercise 5.

EXERCISE 7 **YOUR CULTURE**

Answer the following questions about your country:

- What are the differences between the following facilities in cities and in the countryside?

    housing   leisure facilities   schools
    medical facilities   transport

- Why are facilities different between the city and the countryside?
- Where might these people prefer to live – in a city or in the countryside? Why?

    A couple in their 60s who have just retired

    A young single professional person

    A pensioner who has no family

    A teacher with two teenage children

    A writer with a baby and a toddler

Find information about the standard of living in your country from a website:

Go to a search engine such as **www.google.com** and type in keywords, including the name of your country; e.g.

    "standard of living"+Thailand   "city life"+in modern Taiwan

(Be careful to use + and " " as shown above).

Then choose webpages to read. When you find a useful webpage, print it out.

NB Do not memorise any texts you find. It will not help you in the IELTS examination. Only use the texts for information, for reading practice and to extend your vocabulary.

12 education

UNIT 12

EXERCISE 1   **VOCABULARY**

A   Write the vocabulary in the left-hand column under the correct heading in the chart:

Vocabulary	Educational Institutions
kindergarten	
BA/BSc	
certificate	
PhD	
primary school	**Qualifications**
secondary school	
MA/MSc/MBA	
university	
polytechnic	
diploma	

B   Mark the word stress for the vocabulary in the chart.

C   Put the vocabulary under each heading in order, from most important to least important.

EXERCISE 2   **EDUCATION SYSTEMS**

Read the following text about the education system in Palatonia (a mythical country) and complete the charts that follow:

In Palatonia, all children go to primary school as soon as they are 5 years old. In fact, most of them start school on their birthday. Of course, some of them go to kindie or pre-school as toddlers – from the age of about 2 – but that's optional; compulsory schooling doesn't start until 5 years of age. Primary school is for children aged between 5 and 11 years old. Then they go to secondary school. They can leave when they get to 16 years of age, after they have taken Sixth-form Certificate, but most continue until they are 18 years old, when they sit the University Entrance exam if they want to enter university. An increasing number of both boys and girls go on to tertiary education after that, although tertiary studies are optional, of course. There's a wide range of tertiary institutions to study at – universities and polytechnics, of course, and there are teacher's colleges and lots of private colleges too.

It used to be the case that you could only study for a BA or BSc at a university, but polytechnics now offer a number of bachelor level degree programmes, as well as diplomas and certificates. But to do a post-graduate course you still have to enrol at a university – polytechnics don't offer masters or PhD programmes. Instead, they offer a range of lower level qualifications – certificates and diplomas, especially in vocational subjects such as cooking, computing, mechanical engineering and so on.

In the chart below, write notes:

Educational Institution	Age of pupils/ students	Attendance compulsory or optional	Qualifications
Kindergarten (kindie)/ Pre-school			
Primary School			
Secondary School			
Tertiary institutions (College, Polytechnic, University)			

In the chart below, put a tick or a cross according to where you can obtain the following qualifications:

	Certificate	Diploma	BA/BSc	MA/MSc/MBA	PhD
Polytechnic					
University					

EXERCISE 3 **YOUR EDUCATION SYSTEM**

A Complete the chart below about the education system in your country.

Educational Institution	Age of pupils/ students	Attendance compulsory or optional	Qualifications

B Write about the education system in your country, using information from the chart above.

EXERCISE 4 **SCHOOL SUBJECTS**

A Write a list of primary school subjects and another list of secondary school subjects.

B Why are the subjects taught at primary and secondary schools different?

C Tick your favourite subjects and put a cross next to the subjects you liked least. Decide why you liked and disliked those subjects.

YOUR EDUCATION

A Check the meaning of the following vocabulary and mark the word stress.

rote learning	stress and pressure	expressing personal opinions
homework	continual assessment	large classes
essays	end-of-year exams	streamed classes
projects	assignments	collaborative learning

B Write a paragraph about your own education, using as much of the vocabulary above as possible.

EXERCISE 6 **YOUR CULTURE**

Answer these questions about yourself and your country:

a) What qualifications do you have already? What qualifications do you hope to gain in the future? What are your educational plans for the future?

b) Did you have a good relationship with your teachers/university lecturers? Why/Why not?

c) Would you like to be a teacher/lecturer yourself in the future? Why/why not?

d) How would you change the education system in your country if you could?

e) What percentage of people in your country study at tertiary level? Is it increasing? If so, why?

f) What percentage of people studying at tertiary level in your country are male and what percentage are female? If it is not the same for males and females, why is that?

g) How important is a good education system for a country's economy?

Homework
UNIT 12

Find more information about the education system in your country from an encyclopedia or from one of these websites:

www.usc.edu *(In the 'Search USC' Box, type 'education system' and your country; e.g. education system China, education system Germany, then click on 'Go')*

www.unesco.org/iau/whed.html *(find the name of your country and click on it)*

www.unesco.org *(then click on 'statistics', click on 'country profiles', then click on your country)*

For information about other aspects of the education system in your country, go to a search engine such as **www.google.com** and type in keywords, including the name of your country; e.g.

"primary school education"+"in Japan"　　　"tertiary education"+"in Pakistan"

(Be careful to use + and " " as shown above).

Then choose webpages to read. When you find a useful webpage, print it out.

NB Do not memorise any texts you find. It will not help you in the IELTS examination. Only use the texts for information, for reading practice and to extend your vocabulary.

13 work

EXERCISE 1   **VOCABULARY**

A   Match the vocabulary in the left-hand column with the meanings in the right-hand column below:

Vocabulary	Meanings
is patient	can drive
is persuasive	works well with other people
is authoritative	has new, original ideas
is brave	notices details
is creative	can persuade other people to do things
is multi-lingual	doesn't become angry easily
works well under pressure	is not frightened in dangerous situations
is good with figures	is good at arithmetic
is computer literate	doesn't get stressed easily
is a team player	writes and/or speaks
holds a driver's licence	people listen to this person and do what (s)he says
has an eye for detail	speaks several languages
is a good communicator	knows how to use a computer well

B   Mark the word stress for the nouns and adjectives in the left-hand column above.

C   Memorise the vocabulary and their meanings and then test yourself.

D   Tick the vocabulary above that describe you. Add other information about your characteristics and skills.

EXERCISE 2   **CHARACTERISTICS AND SKILLS**

What characteristics and skills do the people in the left hand column below need to be successful in their jobs? Write the vocabulary from Exercise 1 in the 2 columns below according to your ideas (we have done an example for you):

	Characteristics needed to be successful	Skills needed to be successful
Secretary to company director	is well-organised	is computer literate
Primary school teacher		
Salesman		
Company director		
Firefighter		

EXERCISE 3	**YOUR FUTURE WORK**

Answer these questions about yourself:

A What job would you like to do in the future?

B Write the characteristics and the skills that you will need to be successful in that job.

C Compare your own characteristics and skills (look back at Exercise 1D) with the characteristics and skills you wrote in Exercise 3.B. If they are not the same, what can you do about the differences?

D Write a short paragraph about why you think you would be good at your chosen job, using vocabulary from Exercise 1.

EXERCISE 4 **EMPLOYMENT PRIORITIES**

Different companies offer their employees different benefits. Put the following factors in order of importance for you in your choice of a company to work for. Number them from 1 (most important) to 8 (least important):

> opportunities to travel in your job
>
> a company pension
>
> childcare facilities (e.g. a crèche)
>
> long, paid holidays
>
> free medical insurance
>
> a comfortable working environment
>
> a share in the company profit each year
>
> a company car

EXERCISE 5 **DIFFERENT TYPES OF COMPANIES**

A What would be the pros and cons of working for the following types of company?

Company types: a multinational company   a national company
                    a local company   your own company

B Look at the list of potential work features in the left-hand column below. Write the types of company in your country that are most likely to offer those features in the right-hand column below:

Potential work features	Company type
lots of responsibility	your own company
the potential for international travel	_____
a friendly working environment	_____
a need for English language skills	_____
long holidays	_____
the opportunity for quick promotion	_____
a comfortable working environment	_____
a share in the company profit	_____
a company car	_____
perks such as childcare facilities, medical insurance etc.	_____
a company pension	_____

Write about which types of company you would prefer to work for and why. Include information about potential features.

YOUR CULTURE

In many countries, employment patterns have changed considerably over the last 10 to 20 years. Look at the following statements. Tick any that are true about your country and change others so that they are also true about your country.

  a) Work is becoming more stressful and pressurised.

  b) More and more people are working from home, using computers to do their work and to communicate with their office.

  c) Increasing numbers of women are going out to work.

  d) People are working longer hours but are not being paid more.

  e) Manufacturing industries are employing fewer people because they are becoming automated.

  f) Service industries such as banking, insurance, hospitality and so on are becoming more important for the economy as manufacturing becomes less important.

  g) Companies are introducing flexible work hours so that some employees work from early morning to early afternoon and others work from late morning to late afternoon.

  h) More and more companies are open on a 24/7 basis (i.e. 24 hours a day, 7 days a week).

Homework
UNIT 13

Find more information about companies to suit you from this website:

www.fortune.com/fortune/bestcompanies *(then click on 'Find the Right Company for You', then answer the questions)*

For information about employment in your country, go to a search engine such as **www.google.com** and type in keywords, including the name of your country; e.g.

changes+employment+China   equality+employment+Japan

part-time+employment+Malaysia

(Be careful to use + as shown above).

Then choose webpages to read. When you find a useful webpage, print it out.

NB Do not memorise any texts you find. It will not help you in the IELTS examination. Only use the texts for information, for reading practice and to extend your vocabulary.

UNIT 1   Food – ANSWERS

Exercise 1A

Staple Foods	Countries
bread	France
potatoes	Ireland
rice	China
cassava/manioc	Paraguay
corn	Mexico

Exercise 2B

Deep frying and roasting are probably the least healthy because the foods absorb the oil or fat. Steaming (for vegetables) is probably most healthy because the vitamins are not lost. Grilling (for meat and fish) is probably the most healthy because there is no extra oil or fat.

Exercise 2C

The cooking method is baking, the staple food is potatoes.

Exercise 4A and 4C

Ingredients	Tastes	Foods
sugar, honey	sweet	de´sserts, sweets
chilli	spicy	curries
cheese, butter, cream	rich	cheese sauce, chocolate cake
soya sauce, salt	salty	pickled vegetables
tofu, flour	bland	bread

Exercise 8

There are many possible answers, including:

Food/Drink	Possible health problems
sweet foods	tooth decay, diabetes
spicy foods	stomach ulcers
rich food	obesity, heart disease
salty food	strokes, high blood pressure
soft drinks	hyperactivity, diabetes
alcoholic drinks	liver damage, heart disease

UNIT 1   Food – TEACHER'S NOTES

Ex. 1A   Check that the students know the countries in the right-hand column. Ask them to say what foods they associate with those countries, then ask them to work individually to match the countries and the staple foods, using their dictionaries to check the meaning of the staple foods.

Ex. 1B   Ask them to discuss in small groups the answers to the three questions about their own staple food.

Ex. 2A and 2B   Ask the students to work individually, then to compare their answers in pairs.

Ex. 2C   Read aloud to the students the paragraph about baking potatoes. Tell them to guess the cooking method and the staple food. Elicit their ideas as a class.

Ex. 3   This can be done in class or for homework. When the writing is complete, ask the students to read their description to each other in pairs. They should listen to their partner and decide what cooking method and staple food is being described. Then ask them to exchange their papers. The students read their partner's paper and tick any vocabulary they recognise from the unit. They can then also mark their partner's writing for grammar use, connectives, paragraphing etc.

Ex. 4A and 4B   Ask the students to work individually, then to compare their answers in pairs.

Ex. 4C	Ask the students to work individually, then to compare their answers in new pairs.
Ex. 5A	Ask the students to cover the information in Ex 5b) and to discuss their answers to Ex 5a) in small groups, then ask the groups to write their ideas on the board (notes, not sentences). Ask the students to read the information in b) individually and to check which of the answers on the board was closest to the information in Ex 5b).
Ex. 6	Tell the students to write a short paragraph individually, then ask them to mingle and to read out their paragraphs to each other to try and find another student who has similar likes and dislikes. (Ensure they do not show their paragraphs to each other as this should be a listening exercise, not a reading exercise). Elicit feedback as a class.
Ex. 7	Ask the students to work individually to circle and to tick the drinks that they and their parents (or grandparents, or children) like, then tell them to discuss their responses in small groups.
Ex. 8	Tell the students to work in pairs without dictionaries initially. When they have attempted to discuss their ideas without dictionaries, allow them to use their bilingual dictionaries to find specialist vocabulary.
Ex. 9	Read the sentences aloud for the students to listen to as they also read them in the book silently. Check any vocabulary or comprehension problems after each sentence, but don't discuss if they are true or not. Ask the students to work in pairs to discuss if the sentences are true about their country/countries and to help each other to alter any statements that are not true.
Homework	Give them the homework of looking for information in an encyclopedia or on the web. Tell students that they must work individually, in pairs or in 3s to find an interesting or useful text about food in their culture. They must bring a copy of that text to the next class for other students to read.

NB Emphasise that memorising the text to use it in the IELTS examination is not a good idea.

UNIT 2   Family – ANSWERS

Exercise 1A and 1B	´mother ´father ´brother ´sister ´stepmother ´stepfather ´stepbrother ´stepsister ´mother-in-law ´father-in-law ´brother-in-law ´sister-in-law ´aunt ´uncle ´nephew ´niece ´cousin ´grandmother ´grandfather
Exercise 2	Picture 1 – b, c, f, g Picture 2 – d, f, h Picture 3 – a, g Picture 4 – c, e, g
Exercise 3	´single verb /(adjective) en´gaged (noun / adjective) ´married (noun / adjective) ´separated (noun / adjective) di´vorced (noun / adjective) a´dopt (verb / adjective) ´widow (noun / adjective) ´widower (noun / adjective) ´half-brother (noun / adjective) ´half-sister (noun / adjective)
Exercise 6A	**Word Parts** **Meanings** solo- (e.g. soloist) alone, one bi- (e.g. bicycle) two mono- (e.g. monoplane) one poly- (e.g. polygon) many

Ex. 1A In some languages there are different words for aunts, uncles, etc who are blood relatives and aunts, uncles etc who are relatives by marriage. Decide if 'mother' and 'stepmother' are BR or RM as a class. Ask the students to work individually on the other words, then allow them to compare their ideas in pairs or small groups.

Ex. 1B Ask the students to work individually on marking the word stress, without using a dictionary, then to compare their ideas in pairs (it should be easy as all the items normally have the stress on the first syllable).

Ex. 1C Ask the students to work individually to note the number of BR and RM they have, then ask them to count up their totals individually. Tell them to form a line across the class from the person with the most relatives to the person with the least number of relatives (ensure they discuss the number of relatives they have in order to do this).

Ex. 1D Ask half the class to work in small groups to brainstorm and make notes about the advantages of living in a large family. Ask the other half to work in small groups on the advantages of living in a small family. Elicit feedback as a class.

Ex. 2 Ask the students to work individually, then to compare their answers in pairs. Tell them to decide which of the sentences are true about themselves.

Ex. 3 Ask the students to discuss in small groups the meaning, the pronunciation and the word class of the vocabulary, without using dictionaries. When the students have attempted all the items without dictionaries, allow them to check using dictionaries.

Ex. 4 Ask the students to work individually and then to compare their sentences in groups.

Ex. 5 Ask the students to discuss their ideas in pairs.

Ex. 6 This can be done in class or for homework. Ask the students to write their names on the back of the paper they write on, not on the front. When the writing is complete, collect in the papers, write a number on the front (a different number for each paper) and put the papers round the room. Tell the students to read the different papers and to guess which student wrote each paper; e.g.
Paper 1 – Cherie
Paper 2 – Frank
etc

Ex. 7A Explain that it is not possible to teach every word that the students may need in any exam, so they also need strategies to guess words. Exercise 6 helps by looking at some common 'word parts' (the term used throughout this book for both affixes and word roots). Ask the students to work individually to match the word parts and their meanings, then elicit if they know any other words that start with the same word parts.

Ex. 7B Ask the students to work individually to scan for and underline the word parts. Ensure that students try to guess the meaning of 'bigamy' and 'polygamy'. If necessary, explain to them what 'monogamy' is and then ask them to tell you what 'bigamy' and 'polygamy' mean.

Ex. 8 Ask the students to read through the questions and to underline any vocabulary they do not understand. Elicit any problem vocabulary and check it. Tell them to discuss their answers in small groups.

Homework Give them the homework of checking for information in an encyclopedia or on the web. Tell students that they must work individually, in pairs or in 3s to find out some new fact about family, marriage, divorce, adoption etc in their countries. They must bring that one piece of factual information to the next class.

NB Emphasise that memorising the text to use it in the IELTS examination is not a good idea.

Exercise 1A and 1B

Type of fabric (noun)	Type of clothing (noun)	Style of clothing (adjective)
silk	shirt	short-sleeved
cotton	blouse	polo-neck
wool	suit	full-length
lycra ✔	jacket	V-neck
polyester ✔	skirt	close-fitting
linen	trousers	round neck
nylon ✔	morning suit	long sleeved
down	sweater	flared
viscose ✔	sweatshirt	sleeveless

Exercise 2A

Orange, pale green, dark blue, turquoise, cream etc.

Exercise 5

Casual clothing: silk bowtie
Formal women's clothing: cap
Formal men's clothing: cotton sweatshirt

UNIT 3   Clothing – TEACHER'S NOTES

Ex. 1A and 1B   Ask the students to work individually, then to compare their answers in small groups.

Ex. 1C   Ask the students to work in pairs, then divide the pairs into separate groups of about 3 students and ask them to discuss the clothing they believe is fashionable.

Ex. 2A   Ask the students to work in pairs to think of other colours without using dictionaries. Ask each pair to tell you one colour that they have thought of. If necessary, allow them to use their dictionaries to find more colours.

Ex. 2B   Ask the students to work individually, then to compare their answers in small groups.

Ex. 3   This should be done in class. Ask the students to write about the clothes they are wearing – type, style, colour, and fabric. Ask the students to write their names on the back of the paper they write on, not on the front. Collect in the papers, write a number on the front (a different number for each paper) and put the papers round the room. Tell the students to read the different papers and to guess which student wrote each paper; e.g.
Paper 1 – Cherie
Paper 2 – Frank
etc

Ex. 4   Ask the students to work in pairs to discuss their opinions. Elicit feedback as a class.

Ex. 5   Read aloud the three lists, including the headings. Tell the students to write down the incorrect clothing item in each list. Allow them to compare their answers in pairs.

Ex. 6   Ask the students to work individually to answer the questions, then to compare their answers in pairs.

Ex. 7A   Elicit a list of people who normally wear uniforms in the students' country/countries. Write the list on the whiteboard. Ask the students to look at Ex. 7A to check if their list and the list in the book are the same or different.

Ex. 7B   Copy the list of people who wear uniforms from the board on to separate pieces of paper. Ask the students to work in pairs or in threes and to choose a secretary. Give each pair or group a piece of paper and ask them to write a description of the uniform that the people on the piece of paper wear.

Tell them not to write who the people are. When they have completed their description, ask the secretary in the pair/group to dictate the description to their partner(s) to write down so that each student in the pair or group has their own copy. Divide the pairs or groups into new groups and ask them to read out their descriptions to each other. (Ensure they do not show their writing to each other as this should be a listening exercise, not a reading exercise). Tell them to listen to the descriptions and to guess what group of people wear the uniform being described.

Ex. 7C   Ask the students to work in pairs or small groups. Elicit their ideas as a class.

Ex. 8   If the students are from the same country, ask them to read and think about their answers to the questions, then discuss them as a class. If the students are from different countries, ask them to work individually or in nationality groups to discuss their answers, then mix the nationalities and ask them to tell each other about their answers.

Homework   Give them the homework of looking for information in a tourist guide, an encyclopedia or on the web. Tell students that they must work individually, in pairs or in 3s to find an interesting or useful text about clothing in their culture. They must bring a copy of that text to the next class for other students to read.

NB Emphasise that memorising the text to use it in the IELTS examination is not a good idea.

UNIT 4   Housing – ANSWERS

Exercise 1A

Word Parts	Meanings
single- (e.g. single-minded)	one, only, alone
semi- (e.g. semi-circle)	half under, below
-less (e.g. hopeless)	without
sub- (e.g. substandard)	under, below, less than
urb- (e.g. urban)	city
-ship (e.g. friendship)	noun
multi- (e.g. multi-talented)	many

Exercise 2

Match the following descriptions of types of housing with the pictures below:
a) 5   b) 3   c) 4   d) 2   e) 1

Exercise 3C

very small windows	big picture windows
dark	light
airless	airy
cramped	spacious
low ceilings	high ceilings
cluttered	only a few pieces
old-fashioned	modern

Exercise 5

Areas to live	Building materials	Home ownership
the ´countryside	´stone	to ´rent
´urban ´areas	´concrete	to ´pay a ´mortgage
the ´suburbs	´mud	to ´own
the ´city ´centre	´wood	
	´brick	

NB We use the definite article in '**the** countryside', '**the** suburbs' and '**the** city centre'.

Ex. 1A Explain that it is not possible to teach every word that the students may need in any exam, so they also need strategies to guess words. Exercise 1 helps by looking at some common 'word parts' (the term used throughout this book for both affixes and word roots). Ask the students to cover the right-hand column and to discuss in pairs what they think the word parts mean, without using dictionaries. If necessary, help them with the meanings of the example words in brackets. Then ask them to uncover the right-hand column and to match the word parts with their meanings.

Ex. 1B Give the students 2 minutes to memorise the word parts, the example words and the meanings of the word parts, then ask them to test each other in pairs, taking it in turns to say a word part for their partner to give the meaning and an example word; e.g.

Student 1:   Semi.

Student 2:   Half. Semi-circle.

Ex. 1C Ask the students to work individually to scan for and circle the words.

Ex. 2 Ask the students to work individually.

Ex. 3A Ask the students to work individually, then to compare their answers in pairs or small groups.

Ex. 3B and 3C Ask the students to work individually.

Ex. 4 This can be done in class or for homework. When the writing is complete, ask the students to work in pairs. Tell them to exchange their written descriptions and to read their partner's description for a few minutes. Then ask the students to take it in turns to talk about the information on their home town or city by reading from their notes. Their partner should listen for any differences between the information in the written description that they have read and in the spoken description that they hear.

Ex. 5 Ask the students to work individually, without using dictionaries. Then tell them to compare their answers in pairs. When the students have attempted all the items without dictionaries, allow them to check using dictionaries.

Ex. 6 If the students are from the same country, ask them to read and think about their answers to the questions, then discuss them as a class. If the students are from different countries, ask them to work individually or in nationality groups to discuss their answers, then mix the nationalities and ask them to tell each other about their answers.

Homework Give them the homework of looking for information in an encyclopedia or on the web. Tell students that they must work individually, in pairs or in 3s to find an interesting or useful text about architecture in their country. They must bring a copy of that text to the next class for other students to read.

NB Emphasise that memorising the text to use it in the IELTS examination is not a good idea.

UNIT 5   Pets – ANSWERS

Exercise 1A and 1B	**Vocabulary**	**Opposites**
	res´ponsible (adjective)	irres´ponsible
	´practical (adjective)	im´practical
	a´ffectionate (adjective)	una´ffectionate
	´faithful (adjective)	un´faithful
	de´pendent (adjective)	inde´pendent
	ex´pensive (adjective)	inex´pensive
	´legal (adjective)	i´llegal
	´treat ´well (verb + 'well')	´treat ´badly
	be´have ´well (verb + 'well')	be´have ´badly/ ´misbe´have
	o´bedient (adjective)	diso´bedient
	´easy to ´train ('easy'+ 'to'+ infinitive)	´difficult to ´train/ ´hard to ´train

Exercise 4   There are many possible answers; for example:

Toddlers – fish may be suitable, because

      they do not need to be trained

      they do not bite or scratch

Single working people who live alone – fish and birds may be suitable, because

      they are easy to look after

      they do not need to be taken for a walk, as a dog does

      they will not damage furniture etc, as a dog or cat could

      they do not need to be trained

Young children aged 6-12 – a dog may be suitable, because

      they are usually affectionate and faithful

      they are fun to play with

Elderly people living alone – a cat may be suitable, because

      they are usually affectionate

      they are easy to care for (they do not need to be taken for a walk)

      they are independent

      they are easy to train

      they are inexpensive to feed

UNIT 5   Pets – TEACHER'S NOTES

Ex. 1A and 1B   Ask the students to discuss their ideas in small groups, without using dictionaries. When the students have attempted all the items without dictionaries, allow them to check using dictionaries.

Ex. 1C   Ask the students to work individually to scan for and underline the words.

Ex. 2A and 2B   Discuss the answers as a class.

Ex. 3A   Ask the students to work individually. If the students are from the same country, ask them to talk about their ideas in a pyramid discussion, so that eventually all the students agree on the same order. If the students are from different countries, ask them to compare their answers in pairs or small groups.

Ex. 3B and 3C   Check the meaning and pronunciation of the characteristics vocabulary in Ex 3B as a class, then ask the students to work individually to write the characteristics next to their list of pets. Ask them to discuss in small groups the characteristics they have listed for the different pets.

Ex. 3D   This can be done in class or for homework. Tell the students not to write the type of pet on their paper, but only to describe it. When the writing is complete, ask the students to mingle and to read out their description. (Ensure they do not show their writing to each other as this should be a listening exercise, not a reading exercise). Tell them to listen to the description and to guess the type of pet being described.

Ex. 4   Ask the students to discuss their ideas in pairs or small groups.

Ex. 5A   If the students are from the same country, ask them to work in pairs or small groups. If they are from different countries, ask them to work individually and then to compare their answers in pairs.

Ex. 5B   Discuss the possible solutions as a class.

Ex. 5C   Ask the students to work individually to answer the questions.

Ex. 6   Ask the students to work individually and then to compare their answers in small groups.

Homework   Give them the homework of looking for information in an encyclopedia or on the web. Tell students that they must work individually, in pairs or in 3s to find an interesting or useful text about pets. They must bring a copy of that text to the next class for other students to read.

•NB•   Emphasise that memorising the text to use it in the IELTS examination is not a good idea.

Exercise 1A

Quantity

A large number of (cars)

Quite a number of (cars)

Several (cars)

A few (cars)

One or two (cars)

Exercise 1B iii

Exercise 2A

Places of Worship	Business Premises	Educational Institutions	Child Care Facilities
´synagogue	´office ´block	´secondary ´school	´crèche
´mosque	´shopping ´mall	uni´versity	´kindergarten
´temple	´market	´primary ´school	
´church	´factory		

Exercise 3A

Babies are infants under the age of 12 months.

Toddlers are aged between 1 and 2½ years old.

Teenagers are aged between 13 and 19 years old.

People in their 20s are aged between 20 and 29.

People in their early 30s are aged between 30 and 33.

People in their mid 40s are aged between 44 and 46.

People in their late 50s are aged between 57 and 59.

Middle aged people are between 40 and 60 years old.

Pensioners/retired people have finished working and/or are aged 65 years old.

The elderly are aged over 70 years old.

The word 'child' is generally used about a boy or girl aged between 3 and 12 years old.

The word 'adult' is generally used about someone who is over 18 years of age.

Exercise 4A

Heading 3: Leisure facilities

mus´eums

´cinemas

´opera ´houses

´art ´galleries

´concert ´halls

´theatres

´swimming ´pools

´sports ´stadiums

´parks

UNIT 6 Cities – TEACHER'S NOTES

Ex. 1A and 1B   Ask the students to work individually, then to compare their answers in pairs.

Ex. 2A   Ask the students to work individually to decide on the meaning and word stress of the vocabulary, without using dictionaries. Then tell them to compare their answers in pairs. When the students have attempted all the items without dictionaries, allow them to check using dictionaries.

Ex. 2B   Ask the students to work individually, then to talk about their answers in pairs.

Ex. 2C	Ask the students to imagine the facilities in an imaginary city and list their ideas on the whiteboard; then work as a class to produce a written description on the whiteboard of the imaginary city based on the list of facilities. Reduce the written description to notes by gradually rubbing out sections of the text as the students memorise the entire description. Ask the students to work individually to reproduce the entire written text from memory and from the notes you have left on the board, then allow them to compare their answers in pairs or groups of three.
	In class or for homework, ask the students to write a description of their own home town or city on a piece of paper and also to reduce it to notes on another piece of paper. Tell them to practise saying the information, looking only at their notes.
	When the writing is complete, ask the students to work in pairs. Tell them to exchange their written descriptions and to read their partner's description for a few minutes. Then ask the students to take it in turns to talk about the information on their home town or city by reading from their notes. Their partner should listen for any differences between the information in the written description that they have read and in the spoken description that they hear.
Ex. 2D	Ask the students to work individually, then to discuss their ideas in pairs or small groups.
Ex. 3A	Ask the students to work individually, then to compare their answers in pairs.
	Give the students 3 or 4 minutes to memorise the information, then ask them to test each other in pairs, taking it in turns to read out a sentence up to the age, for their partner to complete; e.g. Student 1. Babies are infants under the age of …. Student 2. 12 months.
Ex. 3B	Ask the students to work individually, then to compare their sentences in groups.
Ex. 4A	Ask the students to work individually, without using dictionaries, then to compare their answers in small groups and to check any problems using their dictionaries.
Ex. 4B and 4C	Ask the students to work individually, then to compare their answers in pairs.
Ex. 4D	This can be done in class or for homework. Tell the students to write on one piece of paper a paragraph about their own preferred leisure facility and to include information about the frequency with which they use the facility and also their reasons for using that facility. Tell them to write the second paragraph about their chosen age group on another piece of paper and to include information on the reasons why that age group uses particular facilities. When the writing is complete, ask the students to mingle to try and find another student with similar preferences in leisure facilities. Tell them to read only their first paragraph to each other. (Ensure they do not show their writing to each other as this should be a listening exercise, not a reading exercise). Elicit feedback as a class.
	Then ask the students to work in pairs. Tell them to exchange their papers with their second paragraph on it. The students read their partner's paper and tick any vocabulary they recognise from the unit. They can then also mark their partner's writing for grammar use, connectives, paragraphing etc.
Ex. 5	If the students are from the same city, ask them to work in pairs or small groups to discuss their ideas. If they are from different cities, ask them to work individually and then to talk about their answers in pairs or small groups.
Homework	Give them the homework of looking for information in a tourist guide book, an encyclopedia or on the web. Tell students that they must work individually, in pairs or in 3s to find an interesting or useful text about facilities in their home town or city (or capital city, if they live in a small village). They must bring a copy of that text to the next class for other students to read.
	NB Emphasise that memorising the text to use it in the IELTS examination is not a good idea.

Exercise 1A and 1B

Vocabulary	Meaning
A ´physical ´game	a game that involves using the body
An indi´vidual ´game	a game for one person or a game in which one person plays against one other person
A com´petitive ´game	a game where you try to beat another team or another person
A ´team ´game	a game with 2 or more teams playing against each other
A ´sedentary ´job	a job that does not involve moving the body
A de´manding ´job	a job that is difficult to do
A ´quadrant	a square divided into 4 smaller squares
The ´least im´portant	the opposite of the most important

Exercise 3A

There is more than one possible order, depending on how energetically you walk or play table tennis. One answer is:

most physical
running
playing table tennis
walking
playing the piano
sewing
watching TV
most sedentary

Exercise 4

All the sentences are true

Exercise 5

There is more than one possible answer because some sports can be in more than one section of the quadrant – e.g. running could be in all sections as it can be non-competitive or competitive and also either an individual or a team sport. However, one answer is:

	Competitive	Non-competitive
Team Sport	football basketball rugby	mountain climbing white water rafting
Individual Sport	swimming running motor racing golf	paragliding bungy jumping skydiving

UNIT 7   Leisure – TEACHER'S NOTES

Ex. 1A and 1B   Ask the students to work individually, without using dictionaries, then tell them to compare their answers in pairs. Allow them to check their ideas using a dictionary.

Ex. 1C   Give the students 2 or 3 minutes to memorise the pronunciation and meaning of the vocabulary, then ask them to test each other in pairs, taking it in turns to read out the definitions for their partners to give the vocabulary, using the correct word stress; e.g.
Student 1:   A square divided into 4 smaller squares.
Student 2:   A ´quadrant.

Ex. 2	Ask the students to work individually, then to mingle to try and find another student with a similar list of leisure activities. (Ensure they do not show their writing to each other as this should be a listening exercise, not a reading exercise). Elicit feedback as a class.
Ex. 3A	Ask the students to work individually, then to compare their answers in small groups.
Ex. 3B	Ask the students to work individually to answer the question, then to make a line across the class from students with the most points at one end to students with the least points at the other end.
Ex. 4	Read the sentences aloud for the students to listen to as they also read them in the book silently. Check any vocabulary or comprehension problems after each sentence, but don't discuss whether they are true or false. Ask the students to work individually to decide if the sentences are true or false, then to compare in pairs.
Ex. 5A	Ask the students to work in small groups and to collaborate in checking the meaning of the sports vocabulary, without using a dictionary. When the students have attempted all the items without dictionaries, allow them to check using dictionaries. Tell them to work in their groups to complete the quadrants.
Ex. 5B	Ask the students to discuss the questions in pairs, then discuss their answers as a class.
Ex. 6	Ask the students to think about their answers individually for a minute, then to discuss them in small groups.
Ex. 7	This can be done in class or for homework. Ask the students to write their names on the back of the paper they write on, not on the front. When the writing is complete, collect in the papers, write a number on the front (a different number for each paper) and put the papers round the room. Tell the students to read the different papers and to guess which student wrote each paper; e.g. Paper 1 – Cherie Paper 2 – Frank etc
Ex. 8	If the students are from the same country, divide the questions between the students in the class so that 2 students are responsible for one or more questions. Then separate the pairs of students into 2 groups so that each groups has a student from each pair. Ask the groups to discuss their answers to the questions. If the students are from different countries, ask them to discuss their answers in pairs.
Homework	Give them the homework of looking for information in a tourist guide book, an encyclopedia or on the web. Tell students that they must work individually, in pairs or in 3s to find an interesting or useful text about sport and leisure activities in their home town, home city or country. They must bring a copy of that text to the next class for other students to read.

NB Emphasise that memorising the text to use it in the IELTS examination is not a good idea.

UNIT 8   Transport – ANSWERS

Exercise 1A and 1B	**Word Parts**	**Meanings**	**Example Words**
	trans-	across	transport, transfer, translate, transmit, transparent
	port-	carry	transport, portable, export, import, porter, support
	bi-	two	bicycle, biannual, bilateral, binoculars, bilingual, bigamy
	inter-	between	intercity, interfere, international, interrupt, interval
	urb-	city	urban, suburban
	mono-	one	monorail, monogamy, monolingual, monotone
	motor-	engine	motorcar, motorised, motorist, motorway, motorbike
	numer-	number	numerous, numerical, numeral
	tri-	three	tricycle, triangle, trilateral, trio, triplet, tripod

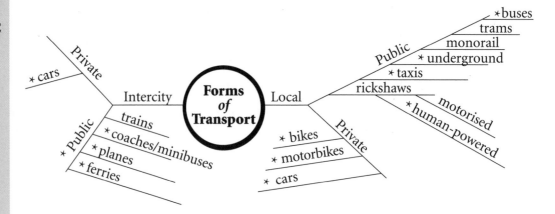

Vocabulary	Meanings
range	variety
options	choices
major	important/large
numerous	very many/a large number
various	different

Adjective	Noun
´comfortable	´comfort
´fast	´speed
ex´pensive	ex´pense
´private	´privacy
´healthy	´health
´easy	´ease
con´venient	con´venience
environ´mental	en´vironment
´safe	´safety

UNIT 8   Transport – TEACHER'S NOTES

Ex. 1A and 1B   Explain that it is not possible to teach every word that the students may need in any exam, so they also need strategies to guess words. Exercise 1 helps by looking at some common 'word parts' (the term used throughout this book for both affixes and word roots). Ask the students to work in groups, without using dictionaries, to think of one word for each of the word parts in the left-hand column. Ask the groups to write their words on the boards, then ask them to work individually to match the word parts with their meanings. Check the matching of the word parts/meanings as a class and then check if the words on the board have the same word part meanings.

Ex. 2A   If the students are from the same home town or city, elicit the different forms of transport as a class and write them up on the board. If the students are from different home towns, ask them to work individually to produce a list of transport forms and then discuss their lists in small groups.

Ex. 2B   Ask the students to work individually to check the list on the board/their own list. Check if anyone's list matched the text exactly or nearly.

Ex. 2C   Ask the students to work individually, then check by drawing the mind map on the board for one or more students to complete.

Ex. 2D   Ask the students to work individually to scan for and underline the vocabulary and then to match the vocabulary with the meanings.

Ex. 3   This can be done in class or for homework. Tell them not to copy the Palatonia text. Ask them to write their name and home town or city at the top of their piece of paper. When the writing is complete, if the students are from the same home town/city, ask them to work in pairs and to compare their mind maps and their writing; if they are from different home towns/cities, put the homework round the room and ask the students to circulate to read the different papers to decide whose country and home town or city has the best range of transport options.

Ex. 4A and 4B Ask the students to work individually, without using dictionaries, then to compare their answers in small groups and to check any problems using their dictionaries.

Ex. 4C Give the students 2 minutes to memorise the vocabulary, including the word stress, then ask them to test each other in pairs, taking it in turns to say a word for their partner to give the word class and then to say the other word and its word class; e.g.
Student 1:   'Easy'.
Student 2:   Adjective; and the noun is 'ease'.

Ex. 5 Ask the students to work individually to number the factors from 1 (most important to them) to 9 (least important to them), then ask them to mingle to try and find other students with the list in the same order. (Ensure they do not show their lists to each other as this should be a listening exercise, not a reading exercise). Elicit feedback as a class.

Ex. 6 Ask the students to work individually to think about their answers to the questions, then tell them to discuss their answers in pairs or small groups, using vocabulary from Exercises 1, 2, 4 and 5.

Homework Give them the homework of looking for information in a guide book, an encyclopedia or on the web. Tell students that they must work individually, in pairs or in 3s to find an interesting or useful text about transport in their home town, home city or country. They must bring a copy of that text to the next class for other students to read.

NB Emphasise that memorising the text to use it in the IELTS examination is not a good idea.

UNIT 9   Traffic – ANSWERS

Exercise 1A

Quantity Expressions (countable nouns)	Quantity Expressions (uncountable nouns)
a large number of (cars)	a great deal of (pollution)
quite a number of (cars)	a fair amount of (pollution)
several (cars)	some (pollution)
a few (cars)	a small amount of (pollution)
no (cars)	no (pollution)

Exercise 2C

Problems	Health effects		Overall effect
Air pollution	respiratory diseases		
Noise pollution	heart disease & high blood pressure	}	negative effect
Traffic congestion	stress & time wasted		on the economy
Traffic accidents	injuries & death		

Exercise 3
a) enable
b) lengthen
c) shorten
d) encourage
e) widen
f) narrow
g) ensure
h) strengthen
i) weaken

Ex. 1A   Ask the students to cover the right-hand column and elicit expressions for uncountable nouns (e.g. 'pollution') to match the expressions in the left-hand column for countable nouns. Write their ideas for uncountable noun quantity expressions on the whiteboard, then ask them to uncover the right-hand column and to put the expressions in order and then to compare their ideas with the expressions in the book. Give the students 3 or 4 minutes to memorise the expressions, then ask them to test each other in pairs, taking it in turns to say a countable expression for their partner to give the equivalent uncountable expression; e.g.
Student 1:   A large number of cars.
Student 2:   A great deal of pollution.

Ex. 1B   Ask the students to work individually.

Ex. 2A and 2B   Ask the students to work individually, then to compare their answers in pairs or small groups.

Ex. 2C   Ask the students to work individually, then to compare their answers in pairs.

Ex. 3   Ask the students to work in teams. The teams try to write the verbs in the left-hand column, without using dictionaries. Ask the students to pass their papers to another team to mark.

Ex. 4A   Read the sentences aloud for the students to listen to as they also read them in the book silently. Check any vocabulary or comprehension problems after each sentence, but don't discuss how effective/useful the ideas are. Ask the students to work individually to put them in order, then to discuss their answers in pairs or small groups.

Ex. 4B   Ask the students to work in pairs, using dictionaries to check any vocabulary they don't understand in the part sentences. Elicit their ideas as a class.

Ex. 5   This can be done in class or for homework. When the writing is complete, ask the students to work in pairs. Tell them to exchange their writing. If they are from the same city, they should read their partner's writing to see if the information is the same as in their own writing. If the students are from different cities, they should read their partner's writing to see what differences there are between their cities. They can then also mark their partner's writing for grammar use, connectives, paragraphing etc.

Ex. 6   Ask the students to work individually and encourage them to guess any answers they don't know. If the students are from the same country, ask them to discuss their ideas as a class. If the students are from different countries, ask them to discuss their answers in small groups.

Homework   Give them the homework of looking for information on the web. Tell students that they must work individually, in pairs or in 3s to find an interesting or useful text about traffic in their home town, home city or capital. They must bring a copy of that text to the next class for other students to read.

NB Emphasise that memorising the text to use it in the IELTS examination is not a good idea.

UNIT 10   Holidays – ANSWERS

Exercise 4A and 4B	**Accommodation**	**Holiday activity**
	ˈbed and ˈbreakfast	ˈvisiting ˈfriends or ˈrelatives
	the ˈhomes of ˈfamily/ ˈfriends	ˈlearning or ˈpractising a ˈhobby (e.g. ski-ing, photography etc.)
	moˈtel	ˈsightseeing
	ˈhostel/ ˈbackpacker's	ˈshopping
	hoˈtel	ˈplaying ˈsports
	ˈcampsite	reˈlaxing on a ˈbeach
	ˈcruise ˈship	

UNIT 10   Holidays – TEACHER'S NOTES

Ex. 1A and 1B   If the students are from the same country, check their ideas as a class. If the students are from different countries, ask them to work individually and then to discuss their answers in pairs.

Ex. 2A   Ask the students to work individually, then to compare their answers in small groups.

Ex. 2B   This can be done in class or for homework. When the writing is complete, ask the students to work in pairs. Tell them to exchange their paragraphs about holiday entitlement. If they are from the same country, they should read their partner's writing to see if the information is the same as in their own writing. If the students are from different countries, they should read their partner's writing to see what differences there are between their countries. They can then also mark their partner's writing for grammar use, connectives, paragraphing etc.

Ex. 3   Ask the students to work individually, then to discuss their answers in small groups.

Ex. 4A and 4B   Ask the students to work individually to decide on the meaning and the word stress of the vocabulary, without using dictionaries. Then tell them to compare their answers in pairs. When the students have attempted all the items without dictionaries, allow them to check using dictionaries if necessary.

Ex. 4C   Elicit any other ideas as a class.

Ex. 5   This can be done in class or for homework. Ask the students to make notes about the information and to practise speaking from their notes. When the notes are complete, tell them to mingle to try and find other students who are interested in a similar holiday. (Ensure they do not show their notes to each other as this should be a listening exercise, not a reading exercise). Elicit feedback as a class.

Ex. 6   Ask the students to work individually to think about their answers to the questions, then tell them to discuss their answers in pairs or small groups, using vocabulary and ideas from the earlier Exercises in the unit.

Homework   Give them the homework of looking for information in a tourist guide book, an encyclopedia or on the web. Tell students that they must work individually, in pairs or in 3s to find an interesting or useful text about holidays, festivals and sightseeing in their culture. They must bring a copy of that text to the next class for other students to read.

NB Emphasise that memorising the text to use it in the IELTS examination is not a good idea.

UNIT 11   Lifestyles – ANSWERS

Exercise 1A and 1B

Vocabulary	Meanings
se´cure (adj.)	safe/unlikely to fail
ex´hausted (adj.)	extremely tired
´nightlife (n.)	evening entertainment (e.g. nightclubs, cinema etc)
´pace (n.)	speed
´sense of com´munity (n.p.)	feeling of loyalty and support between people in a group
´crime ´rate (n.)	the number of crimes
´housing (n.)	accommodation
´status (n.)	social or professional position
´salary (n.)	the pay that professional people receive for their work
´stress (n.)	pressure/emotional strain
´quality of ´life (n.p.)	how enjoyable life is
´standard of ´living (n.p.)	the way people live, based on what they can afford

Exercise 2   a) The person in text 1 has a high standard of living, but the person in text 2 has a better quality of life.

Exercise 5

I used to live in Tupu, Palatonia. It's a very large city and has all the things you might expect in such a large city. One of the positive things is the large **1** <u>shopping malls</u> that are open 24 hours a day, so you can buy anything you want whenever you want; and the different entertainment options – Tupu has a really **2** <u>exciting nightlife</u>. On the negative side, there is terrible **3** <u>pollution</u> because of all the cars; and there are terrible **4** <u>traffic jams</u> at rush hour – everyone complains about the **5** <u>long travel times to work</u> every morning. A great many people move from the countryside into Tupu because there's a wide **6** <u>variety of jobs</u> available in the city, but a lot of these people don't have the necessary skills. When they can't find a job, they turn to crime as a way of getting money. All-in-all, living in the city can be very **7** <u>stressful</u>.

So, about 2 years ago, I moved to a village in the countryside about 70 kms outside Tupu. Life there is completely different. Of course, the **8** <u>pace of life</u> is much slower, but that means people have time to talk to each other; and because everyone knows everyone else in the village they help each other - there is a real **9** <u>sense of community</u>. We don't have a police station in the village and people don't worry about locking their doors when they go out because there is a very **10** <u>low crime rate</u>. And we have **11** <u>clean air</u> due to the small number of cars. All that makes it a very **12** <u>healthy and safe environment</u> for children to grow up in. Although I miss Tupu's nightlife, it does have one advantage – I spend much less money than when I was living in the city; so the low **13** <u>cost of living</u> in the countryside makes it easy to live on a small salary!

UNIT 11 Lifestyles – TEACHER'S NOTES

Ex. 1A and 1B Ask the students to cover the right-hand column and to discuss in pairs the meaning, the word stress and the word class of the vocabulary in the left-hand column, without using dictionaries. Then ask them to uncover the right-hand column and to match the vocabulary with their definitions, still without using dictionaries.

Ex. 1C Give the students 2 or 3 minutes to memorise the vocabulary, including the meaning, the word stress and the word class, then ask them to test each other in pairs, taking it in turns to say a definition for their partner to give the vocabulary and its word class; e.g.
Student 1:   The pay professional people receive for their work.
Student 2:   ´Salary. Noun.

Ex. 2 Check the students understand the meaning of 'standard of living' and 'quality of life'. Ask them to read the texts individually to answer questions a) and b), then to discuss their answers in pairs.

Ex. 3A and 3B Ask the students to work individually to put the points in Exercise 3A in order of priority for them, then to think about their answer to Exercise 3B. Ask them to discuss their answers to Exercises 3A and B in small groups.

Ex. 4 This can be done in class or for homework. When the writing is complete, ask them to mingle and to read out their paragraphs to each other to try and find another student who has similar priorities. (Ensure they do not show their paragraphs to each other as this should be a listening exercise, not a reading exercise). Elicit feedback as a class.

Ex. 5 Ask the students to discuss in pairs the meaning of the vocabulary, without using dictionaries. When the students have attempted all the items without dictionaries, allow them to check using dictionaries. Ask them to fill in the gaps individually.

Ex. 6 This can be done in class or for homework. Ask the students to work individually to write the description. If the students are from the same home town or city, in a following lesson ask them to work in pairs. Tell them to exchange their written descriptions and to read their partner's description for a few minutes. They should read their partner's writing to see if there are any differences of information between their own and the partner's writing.

If the students are from different home towns or cities, ask them to write their name and the name of their home town or city on the front of their papers. When the writing is complete, collect in the papers and put them round the room. Tell the students to read the different papers and to decide which student's home town or city they would most like to live in, which students' home town or city they would least like to live in, and why.

Ex. 7 Ask the students to discuss their answers in small groups.

Homework Give them the homework of looking for information on the web. Tell students that they must work individually, in pairs or in 3s to find an interesting or useful text about the standard of living or quality of life in their country. They must bring a copy of that text to the next class for other students to read.

NB Emphasise that memorising the text to use it in the IELTS examination is not a good idea.

UNIT 12 Education – ANSWERS

Exercise 1A, 1B and 1C

Vocabulary	Educational Institutions
kindergarten BA/BSc certificate PhD primary school secondary school MA/MSc/MBA university polytechnic diploma	′kindergarten ′primary ′school ′secondary ′school poly′technic uni′versity
	Qualifications
	cer′tificate di′ploma BA/BSc MA/MSc/MBA PhD

Exercise 2

Educational Institution	Age of pupils/ students	Attendance compulsory or optional	Qualifications
Kindergarten (kindie)/ Pre-school	About 2 to 5	Optional	None
Primary School	5 to 11	Compulsory	None
Secondary School	11 to 16 16 to 18	Compulsory Optional	Sixth-form certificate University Entrance exam
Tertiary institutions (College, Polytechnic, University)	Over 18	Optional	Certificates, diplomas, bachelor level degrees (BA/ BSc), post graduate degrees (MA/MSc/MBA and PhD)

	Certificate	Diploma	BA/BSc	MA/MSc/MBA	PhD
Polytechnic	✔	✔	✔	x	x
University	x	x	✔	✔	✔

Exercise 6

′rote ′learning	′stress and ′pressure	expressing ′personal o′pinions
′homework	′continual a′ssessment	′large ′classes
′essays	′end-of-′year ex′ams	′streamed ′classes
′projects	a′ssignments	co′llaborative ′learning

Ex. 1A and 1B   Ask the students to work individually to put the vocabulary under the correct headings and to mark the word stress, without using dictionaries. Then tell them to compare their answers in pairs. When the students have attempted all the items without dictionaries, allow them to check using dictionaries.

Ex. 1C   Ask the students to work individually, then to compare their answers in small groups.

Ex. 2   Ask the students to work individually and then to compare their answers in pairs.

Ex. 3A   If the students are from the same country, ask them to work individually to complete the chart, then to compare their charts in pairs. If the students are from different countries, ask them to work individually to complete their chart.

Ex. 3B   This can be done in class or for homework. Ask the students to work individually to write the description but tell them to make 2 or 3 information mistakes in their writing; for example, if their notes in the chart say that attendance at high school is compulsory, they might say in their writing that it is optional.

When the writing is complete, ask the students to work in pairs. Tell them to exchange their written descriptions and to read their partner's description for a few minutes. Then ask the students to take it in turns to talk about the information on their country's education system by reading from their notes in the chart. Their partner should listen for any differences between the information in the written description that they have read and in the spoken description that they hear.

Ex. 4A   Ask the students to work in groups with 1 person acting as secretary to write down the group's list of subjects under the 2 headings 'primary school subjects' and 'secondary school subjects'. Tell the secretaries that they must write legibly as other students will be reading their lists. Give the groups 5 or 6 minutes to brainstorm as many subjects under each heading as they can. (It may be necessary to play background music so that the groups cannot hear each other's ideas). Then tell the students to put their pens/pencils down and to pass their papers clockwise to the next group, who have 1 minute to read the other group's list and to memorise any subjects that they do not have on their own list. (Do not allow them to write anything down.) Pass the papers clockwise again for the groups to read a new paper and to memorise any further new subjects. Continue passing the papers until they are back with their original authors. Allow the groups to add to their own list any subjects they have memorized from the other papers. Find out which group has the largest number of subjects under each heading. Check the spelling and the meaning of any suspect subject names.

Ex. 4B   Discuss their ideas as a class.

Ex. 4C   Ask the students to compile a list of the 3 secondary school subjects they liked most and the 3 secondary school subjects they liked least, and to decide why they liked or disliked those subjects. Ask them to mingle to try and find another student with the same or similar favourite subjects and least favourite subjects and to discuss with them why they liked or disliked those subjects. (Ensure they do not show their list of subjects to each other as this should be a listening exercise, not a reading exercise). Elicit feedback as a class.

Ex. 5A   Ask the students to work in small groups and to collaborate in checking the meaning and word stress of the vocabulary, without using a dictionary. When the students have attempted all the items without dictionaries, allow them to check using dictionaries.

Ex. 5B   This can be done in class or for homework. Ask the students to work individually to write about their own education. When the writing is complete, ask the students to work in pairs. Tell them to take it in turns to read out their writing. Their partner should listen for any similarities or differences between their own education and their partner's education. When they have both read out their writing, they should discuss the similarities and differences. Elicit feedback as a class.

Ex. 6   Ask the students to work individually to answer the questions, then to discuss their answers in small groups.

Homework   Give them the homework of looking for information in an encyclopedia or on the web. Tell students that they must work individually, in pairs or in 3s to find an interesting or useful text about education in their country. They must bring a copy of that text to the next class for other students to read.

NB   Emphasise that memorising the text to use it in the IELTS examination is not a good idea.

UNIT 13   Work – ANSWERS

Exercise 1A and 1B

Vocabulary	Definitions
is ´patient	doesn't become angry easily
is per´suasive	can persuade other people to do things
is au´thoritative	people listen to this person and do what (s)he says
is ´brave	is not frightened in dangerous situations
is cre´ative	has new, original ideas
is ´multi-´lingual	speaks several languages
works ´well under ´pressure	doesn't get stressed easily
is ´good with ´figures	is good at arithmetic
is com´puter ´literate	knows how to use a computer
is a ´team ´player	works well with other people
holds a ´driver's ´licence	can drive
has an ´eye for ´detail	notices details
is a ´good co´mmunicator	writes and/or speaks well

Exercise 2

There are many possible answers, depending on the particular job (for example, some salesmen may need to hold a driver's licence, others may not). One possible answer is:

	Characteristics needed to be successful	Skills needed to be successful
Secretary to company director	is well-organised	is computer literate has an eye for detail is multi-lingual
Primary school teacher	is patient	is a team player
Salesman	is persuasive	is a good communicator is good with figures
Company director	is authoritative	is a good communicator works well under pressure is multi-lingual
Firefighter	is brave	works well under pressure is a team player

Exercise 5B

There is no correct answer as it depends on

- the type of business (e.g. import/export, insurance, manufacturing etc.)
- each employee's particular job
- each individual company's policies
- the country where the company is
- the other people working in the company
  etc.

UNIT 13   Work – TEACHER'S NOTES

Ex. 1A and 1B

Ask the students to work individually to match the vocabulary with the meanings and to mark the word stress on the nouns and adjectives, without using dictionaries. Then tell them to compare their answers in pairs. When the students have attempted all the items without dictionaries, allow them to check using dictionaries.

Ex. 1C

Give the students 3 minutes to memorise the vocabulary, the pronunciation and the meanings, then ask them to test each other in pairs, taking it in turns to say a meaning for their partner to give the vocabulary; e.g.
Student 1:   Works well with other people.
Student 2:   Is a ´team ´player.

Ex. 1D   Ask the students to work individually, then to mingle to try and find another student with a similar list of characteristics and skills. (Ensure they do not show their papers to each other as this should be a listening exercise, not a reading exercise). Elicit feedback as a class.

Ex. 2   Ask the students to work in pairs to complete the chart.

Ex. 3A and 3B   Ask the students to discuss in pairs the jobs they would like to do and the characteristics and skills needed to be successful in the job.

Ex. 3C   Ask the students to work in pairs to compare their own characteristics and skills with the lists they produce for Ex 3B.

Ex. 3D   This can be done in class or for homework. Ask the students to work individually to write about their partner from Ex 3A, B and C. When the writing is complete, tell them to exchange their writing and to read what their partner has written about them. Then ask the students to tell their partners if there are any inaccuracies in the information. They can then also mark their partner's writing for grammar use, connectives, paragraphing etc.

Ex. 4   Ask the students to work individually to number the benefits from 1 (most important to them) to 8 (least important to them), then ask them to mingle to try and find other students with the list in the same order. (Ensure they do not show their lists to each other as this should be a listening exercise, not a reading exercise). Elicit feedback as a class.

Ex. 5A   Ask the students to discuss their ideas in small groups.

Ex. 5B   Ask the students to work individually, then to compare their answers in small groups.

Ex. 6   This can be done in class or for homework. Ask the students to work individually to write about the type of company they would prefer to work for. When the writing is complete, tell them to exchange their writing and to read what their partner has written. Then ask them to make notes from their partner's writing. Divide the pairs into separate groups of about 3 students and ask them to tell each other about their partner's writing, speaking only from their notes.

Ex. 7   Read the sentences aloud for the students to listen to as they also read them in the book silently. Check any vocabulary or comprehension problems after each sentence, but don't discuss them. If the students are from the same country, ask them to work in pairs or small groups. If they are from different countries, ask them to work individually and then to discuss their answers in pairs. Elicit feedback as a class.

Homework   Give them the homework of looking for information on the web. Tell students that they must work individually, in pairs or in 3s to find an interesting or useful text about employment in their country. They must bring a copy of that text to the next class for other students to read.

    NB Emphasise that memorising the text to use it in the IELTS examination is not a good idea.